soup bowl

Vegetable Stock

Makes about $8^3/_4$ cups

Ingredients

2 tbsp sunflower or corn oil

scant $^1/_2$ cup finely chopped onion

scant $^1/_2$ cup finely chopped leek

$^2/_3$ cup finely chopped carrots

4 celery stalks, finely chopped

$^3/_4$ cup finely chopped fennel

1 small tomato, finely chopped

10 cups water

1 bouquet garni

Heat the oil in a large saucepan. Add the onion and leek and cook over low heat, stirring occasionally, for 5 minutes, until softened. Add the remaining vegetables, cover, and cook for 10 minutes. Add the water and bouquet garni, bring to a boil, and simmer for 20 minutes.

Strain the stock into a bowl, let cool, cover, and store in the refrigerator. Use immediately or freeze in portions for up to 3 months.

Fish Stock

Makes about $5^2/_3$ cups

Ingredients

1 lb 7 oz/650 g white fish heads, bones, and
    trimmings, rinsed

1 onion, sliced

2 celery stalks, chopped

1 carrot, sliced

1 bay leaf

4 fresh parsley sprigs

4 black peppercorns

$^1/_2$ lemon, sliced

$5^2/_3$ cups water

$^1/_2$ cup dry white wine

Cut out and discard the gills from any fish heads, then place the heads, bones, and trimmings in a saucepan. Add all the remaining ingredients and gradually bring to a boil, skimming off the foam that rises to the surface. Partially cover and simmer for 25 minutes.

Strain the stock without pressing down on the contents of the sieve. Leave to cool, cover, and store in the refrigerator. Use immediately or freeze in portions for up to 3 months.

Essential Equipment

The beauty of making soup is that it doesn't require lots of special equipment. All you will need to get started are a large, heavy-bottom saucepan and a few basic kitchen items—such as a sharp knife, a cutting board, a slotted spoon or ladle, a wooden spoon, and measuring cups—many of which you probably already have. A blender or food processor is handy for making smooth soups, but as a cheaper alternative you can use a stick blender. This useful piece of equipment allows you to blend your soup right in the saucepan, thus cutting down on washing up.

Key Ingredients

It is said that the base of a good soup is its stock, but you can get by with water if you are using lots of really fresh and tasty ingredients. You can make your own stock—you will find recipes for vegetable, fish, chicken, and beef stocks on the following pages—but it's not a requirement. You can buy good quality ready-prepared stock in aseptic boxes or in cans. Or you can use bouillon cubes, which come in meat, fish, and vegetable flavors and are great to use when a soup needs a very specific taste. Some bouillon cubes have a very concentrated flavor and are best used at half their strength so that they are not too salty. Bouillon powder can also be handy, as you can use it by the spoonful and adjust the flavor and saltiness according to taste. Finally, ready-prepared fresh stock is available from most large supermarkets, although it tends to be quite expensive.

That said, the best stock is the one you make yourself, using simple and wholesome ingredients. Here are a few tips:
• Use the freshest ingredients possible.
• When preparing the stock, make sure the water stays at a simmer; boiling will result in a cloudy stock.
• Skim any foam from the top of the stock so that it stays clear.
• Strain the stock through a sieve to remove any unwanted vegetables and herbs.

• You can reduce the stock by boiling it at the end for a more concentrated flavor. This is particularly useful if you intend to freeze the stock, as you will have a smaller volume to store.
• Allow the stock to cool before using so you can remove any excess fat from the surface.

Vegetables play an important role in soup making. Root vegetables, such as parsnips, carrots, and potatoes, are important for adding bulk. Bulbs like onions, shallots, garlic, and leeks add great flavor. Peas and beans can be puréed or added whole to soups to provide color and flavor. Zucchini and winter squash such as pumpkins are incredibly prolific when in season, so you can make use of their abundance in your soups. Vegetable fruits—this term covers tomatoes, avocados, and bell peppers—all make delicious summer soups. Always make sure that you use vegetables at the peak of their freshness.

Meat is found in various guises in soup making. Bacon is particularly useful for adding flavor, as are sausages, especially the spicy varieties. One advantage of the slow cooking techniques employed in soup-making is that cheaper cuts of meat can be used, resulting in melt-in-your-mouth tender meat and flavorful stock. Chickens—either whole or cut up—can be used for stock, with the meat served separately or cut into smaller pieces and served as part of the soup.

Fish and seafood of all varieties can be used to make tasty soups and chowders. Cod, salmon, squid, mussels, clams, shrimp, crab, lobster, and oysters all work well. Sometimes a selection of fish is served together, as in the French classic, Bouillabaisse.

Finally, don't forget dairy products! A little cream, crème fraîche, or yogurt stirred in just before serving produces a soup with a lovely creamy texture. Using butter instead of oil will add flavor to your soups. Always keep a small piece of cheddar or Parmesan cheese handy for grating and sprinkling over your soup just before serving.

Introduction

If you cook nothing else, you could live exceptionally well on the rich variety of soups you will find in this easy-to-use book.

In many ways, soup is simple. It is either thin, as in consommé, or thick, either puréed or left chunky. This means that soups can be served in a variety of ways—thinner broths make perfect appetizers or healthy snacks, while more robust soups incorporating fish, meat, or vegetables can be meals in themselves. For even more diversity, some soups can even be served cold as well as hot—delicious on a hot summer's day.

There are many styles of soup using a huge variety of ingredients, with many countries having their own traditional favorites—dishes that are firmly entrenched in that nation's culinary history. To name just a few, think of Spanish Gazpacho and Greek Avgolemono, Italian Minestrone, and Ribollita, even Scottish Cullen Skink and Cock-a-Leekie. Farther east there are spicy Middle Eastern recipes and Indian lentil-based dals. In the Far East, Thai flavors contrast with the blander Japanese Miso broth. Watch out for Bird's Nest Soup or Shark's Fin Soup when in China!

Soup making can be exciting and challenging, but don't be put off—all soups have three things in common, which makes them simple to understand and explore.

First, soup is very easy to make. Almost all soups start with sautéing an onion with a tasty vegetable like leek or celery to build a flavor base. You simply add an appropriate stock, together with the main ingredients of your choice, and cook for long enough to soften the vegetables and bring out the flavors. It really couldn't be simpler!

Second, homemade soup is healthy. You can guarantee the quality of the raw ingredients, making sure that you are eating them in season and at the peak of their flavor. Usually there is very little fat involved and you can use the minimum amount of salt, which is why homemade soups are so much better for you than most commercially produced varieties.

Third, soup is so convenient. It is ideal—fresh, or quickly thawed from the freezer—for a quick meal or impromptu dinner party at home, and it only needs a simple bowl for serving. It is easily portable too—just pack it into a Thermos and you can enjoy a delicious cup of soup wherever and whenever you like.

CONTENTS

Love Food ® is an imprint of Parragon Books Ltd

Parragon
Queen Street House
4 Queen Street
Bath, BA1 1HE, UK

ISBN: 978-1-4075-3140-3

Printed in Indonesia

Photography by Mike Cooper
Food styling by Carole Handslip and Sumi Glass

Notes for the reader
• This book uses imperial, metric, and US cup measurements. Follow the same units of measurement throughout, do not mix imperial and metric.
• All spoon measurements are level: teaspoons are assumed to be 5 ml, and tablespoons are assumed to be 15 ml.
• Unless otherwise stated, milk is assumed to be whole, eggs and individual vegetables are medium, and pepper is freshly ground black pepper. The times given are an approximate guide only.
• Some recipes contain nuts. If you are allergic to nuts you should avoid using them and any products containing nuts. Recipes using raw or very lightly cooked eggs should be avoided by infants, the elderly, pregnant women, convalescents, and anyone with a chronic condition.

soup bowl

An inspiring collection of soups, broths, and chowders

Chicken Stock

Makes about $11^{1}/_{4}$ cups

Ingredients

3 lb/1.3 kg chicken wings and necks

2 onions, cut into wedges

$17^{1}/_{2}$ cups water

2 carrots, coarsely chopped

2 celery stalks, coarsely chopped

10 fresh parsley sprigs

4 fresh thyme sprigs

2 bay leaves

10 black peppercorns

Put the chicken wings and necks and the onions in a large saucepan and cook over low heat, stirring frequently, until lightly browned.

Add the water and stir well to scrape off any sediment from the bottom of the pan. Gradually bring to a boil, skimming off the foam that rises to the surface. Add all the remaining ingredients, partially cover, and simmer for 3 hours.

Strain the stock into a bowl, let cool, cover, and store in the refrigerator. When cold, remove and discard the layer of fat from the surface. Use immediately or freeze in portions for up to 6 months.

Beef Stock

Makes about $7^{1}/_{2}$ cups

Ingredients

2 lb 4 oz/1 kg beef marrow bones, cut into
   3-inch/7.5-cm pieces

1 lb 7 oz/650 g braising beef in a single piece

$12^{1}/_{2}$ cups water

4 cloves

2 onions, halved

2 celery stalks, coarsely chopped

8 black peppercorns

1 bouquet garni

Place the bones in the base of a large saucepan and put the meat on top. Add the water and gradually bring to a boil, skimming off the foam that rises to the surface.

Press a clove into each onion half and add to the pan with the celery, peppercorns, and bouquet garni. Partially cover and simmer for 3 hours. Remove the meat and simmer for 1 hour more.

Strain the stock into a bowl, let cool, cover, and store in the refrigerator. When cold, remove and discard the layer of fat from the surface. Use immediately or freeze in portions for up to 6 months.

1

Classic Soups

In this chapter you will find all your old favorites, such as Tomato Soup and Chicken Noodle Soup, along with some more sophisticated combinations, including Creamy Carrot & Parsnip Soup and Clam & Corn Chowder. There is nothing more welcoming than coming home to the aroma of freshly made soup, and these familiar favorites are sure to be a hit with the whole family.

Tomato Soup

Melt half the butter in a saucepan. Add the onion and cook over low heat, stirring occasionally, for 5–6 minutes until softened. Add the tomatoes and bay leaf and cook, stirring occasionally, for 15 minutes, or until pulpy.

Meanwhile, melt the remaining butter in another saucepan. Add the flour and cook, stirring continuously, for 1 minute. Remove the pan from the heat and gradually stir in the milk. Return to the heat, season with salt and pepper, and bring to a boil, stirring continuously. Continue to cook, stirring, until smooth and thickened.

When the tomatoes are pulpy, remove the pan from the heat. Discard the bay leaf and pour the tomato mixture into a food processor or blender. Process until smooth, then push through a fine strainer into a clean saucepan. Bring the tomato purée to a boil, then gradually stir it into the milk mixture. Season with salt and pepper to taste. Ladle into warmed bowls, garnish with basil, and serve immediately.

SERVES 4

$^1/_4$ cup butter

1 small onion, finely chopped

1 lb/450 g tomatoes, coarsely chopped

1 bay leaf

3 tbsp all-purpose flour

$2^1/_2$ cups milk

salt and pepper

sprigs of fresh basil, to garnish

Chunky Vegetable Soup

Put the carrots, onion, garlic, potatoes, celery, mushrooms, tomatoes, and stock into a large saucepan. Stir in the bay leaf and herbs. Bring to a boil, then reduce the heat, cover, and let simmer for 25 minutes.

Add the corn and cabbage and return to a boil. Reduce the heat, cover, and simmer for 5 minutes, or until the vegetables are tender. Remove and discard the bay leaf. Season with pepper to taste.

Ladle into warmed bowls, garnish with basil, if using, and serve immediately.

SERVES 6

2 carrots, sliced

1 onion, diced

1 garlic clove, crushed

12 oz/350 g new potatoes, diced

2 celery stalks, sliced

4 oz/115 g button mushrooms, quartered

14 oz/400 g canned chopped tomatoes

$2^1/_2$ cups Vegetable Stock (see page 10)

1 bay leaf

1 tsp dried mixed herbs or 1 tbsp chopped fresh mixed herbs

$^1/_2$ cup corn kernels, frozen or canned, drained

2 oz/55 g green cabbage, shredded

pepper

sprigs of fresh basil, to garnish (optional)

Minestrone

Heat the oil in a large saucepan. Add the garlic, onions, and prosciutto and cook over medium heat, stirring, for 3 minutes, until slightly softened. Add the red and orange bell peppers and the chopped tomatoes and cook for an additional 2 minutes, stirring. Stir in the stock, then add the celery, beans, cabbage, peas, and parsley. Season with salt and pepper. Bring to a boil, then reduce the heat and simmer for 30 minutes.

Add the vermicelli to the pan. Cook for another 10–12 minutes, or according to the package directions. Remove from the heat and ladle into warmed bowls. Garnish with freshly grated Parmesan cheese and serve immediately.

SERVES 4

2 tbsp olive oil

2 garlic cloves, chopped

2 red onions, chopped

$2^3/_4$ oz/75 g prosciutto, sliced

1 red bell pepper, seeded and
   chopped

1 orange bell pepper, seeded and
   chopped

14 oz/400 g canned chopped
   tomatoes

4 cups Vegetable Stock
   (see page 10)

1 celery stalk, trimmed and sliced

14 oz/400 g canned borlotti beans,
   drained

$3^1/_2$ oz/100 g green leafy cabbage,
   shredded

$2^3/_4$ oz/75 g frozen peas, thawed

1 tbsp chopped fresh parsley

$2^3/_4$ oz/75 g dried vermicelli

salt and pepper

freshly grated Parmesan cheese,
   to garnish

Leek & Potato Soup

Melt the butter in a large saucepan over medium heat, add the onion, leeks, and potatoes, and sauté gently for 2–3 minutes, until softened but not browned. Pour in the stock, bring to a boil, then reduce the heat and simmer, covered, for 15 minutes.

Transfer the mixture to a food processor or blender and process until smooth. Return to the rinsed-out pan.

Reheat the soup, season with salt and pepper to taste, and serve in warmed bowls, swirled with the cream, if using, and garnished with chives.

SERVES 4–6

$^1/_4$ cup butter

1 onion, chopped

3 leeks, sliced

8 oz/225 g potatoes, cut into $^3/_4$-inch/2-cm cubes

$3^1/_2$ cups Vegetable Stock (see page 10)

salt and pepper

$^2/_3$ cup light cream, to serve (optional)

2 tbsp snipped fresh chives, to garnish

French Onion Soup

Thinly slice the onions. Heat the oil in a large, heavy-bottom saucepan over medium–low heat, add the onions, and cook, stirring occasionally, for 10 minutes, or until they are just beginning to brown. Stir in the chopped garlic, sugar, and chopped thyme, then reduce the heat and cook, stirring occasionally, for 30 minutes, or until the onions are golden brown.

Sprinkle in the flour and cook, stirring continuously, for 1–2 minutes. Stir in the wine. Gradually stir in the stock and bring to a boil, skimming off any foam that rises to the surface, then reduce the heat and simmer for 45 minutes.

Meanwhile, preheat the broiler to medium. Toast the bread on both sides under the broiler, then rub the toast with the cut edges of the halved garlic clove.

Ladle the soup into 6 ovenproof bowls set on a baking sheet. Float a piece of toast in each bowl and divide the grated cheese among them. Place under the broiler for 2–3 minutes, or until the cheese has just melted. Garnish with thyme sprigs and serve immediately.

SERVES 6

1 lb 8 oz/675 g onions

3 tbsp olive oil

4 garlic cloves, 3 chopped and 1 peeled and halved

1 tsp sugar

2 tsp chopped fresh thyme, plus extra sprigs to garnish

2 tbsp all-purpose flour

$\frac{1}{2}$ cup dry white wine

$8\frac{1}{2}$ cups Vegetable Stock (see page 10)

6 slices French bread

$10\frac{1}{2}$ oz/300 g Gruyère cheese, grated

Creamy Mushroom & Tarragon Soup

Melt half the butter in a large saucepan. Add the onion and cook gently for 10 minutes, until soft. Add the remaining butter and the mushrooms and cook for 5 minutes, or until the mushrooms are browned.

Stir in the stock and tarragon, bring to a boil, then reduce the heat and simmer gently for 20 minutes. Transfer to a food processor or blender and process until smooth. Return the soup to the rinsed-out pan.

Stir in the sour cream and add salt and pepper to taste. Reheat the soup gently until hot. Ladle into warmed serving bowls and garnish with chopped tarragon. Serve at once.

SERVES 4–6

3 tbsp butter

1 onion, chopped

1 lb 9 oz/700 g button mushrooms, coarsely chopped

$3^1/_2$ cups Vegetable Stock (see page 10)

3 tbsp chopped fresh tarragon, plus extra to garnish

$^2/_3$ cup sour cream

salt and pepper

Cauliflower Soup

Heat the olive oil and butter in a large saucepan and cook the onion and leeks for 10 minutes, stirring frequently, taking care not to let the vegetables color.

Cut the cauliflower into florets and cut the stalk into small pieces. Add to the pan and sauté with the other vegetables for 2–3 minutes.

Add the stock and bring to a boil, cover, and simmer over medium heat for 20 minutes.

Pour the soup into a food processor or blender, process until smooth, and return to the rinsed-out pan.

Heat the soup through, season with salt and pepper to taste, and serve in warmed bowls topped with a spoonful of grated cheese and a drizzle of extra virgin olive oil.

SERVES 6

1 tbsp olive oil

2 tbsp butter

1 large onion, coarsely chopped

2 leeks, sliced

1 large head of cauliflower

$3^3/_4$ cups Vegetable Stock
  (see page 10)

salt and pepper

finely grated cheddar cheese and
  extra virgin olive oil, to serve

Speedy Broccoli Soup

Cut the broccoli into florets and set aside. Cut the thicker broccoli stalks into $1/2$-inch/1-cm dice and put into a large saucepan with the leek, celery, garlic, potato, stock, and bay leaf. Bring to a boil, then reduce the heat, cover, and let simmer for 15 minutes.

Add the broccoli florets to the soup and return to a boil. Reduce the heat, cover, and let simmer for an additional 3–5 minutes, or until the potato and broccoli stalks are tender.

Remove from the heat and let the soup cool slightly. Remove and discard the bay leaf. Purée the soup, in small batches, in a food processor until smooth.

Return the soup to the pan and heat through thoroughly. Season with pepper to taste. Ladle the soup into warmed bowls and serve at once with crusty bread or croutons.

SERVES 6

12 oz/350 g broccoli

1 leek, sliced

1 celery stalk, sliced

1 garlic clove, crushed

12 oz/350 g potatoes, diced

4 cups Vegetable Stock
   (see page 10)

1 bay leaf

pepper

crusty bread or Croutons
   (see page 236), to serve

Watercress Soup

Remove the leaves from the stalks of the watercress and set aside. Coarsely chop the stalks.

Melt the butter in a large saucepan over medium heat, add the onions, and cook for 4–5 minutes, until softened. Do not brown.

Add the potatoes to the pan and mix well with the onions. Add the watercress stalks and the stock.

Bring to a boil, then reduce the heat, cover, and simmer for 15–20 minutes, until the potato is soft.

Add the watercress leaves and stir in to heat through. Remove from the heat and transfer to a food processor or blender. Process until smooth and return the soup to the rinsed-out pan. Reheat and season with salt and pepper to taste, adding a good grating of nutmeg, if using.

Serve in warmed bowls with the yogurt spooned on top and an extra grating of nutmeg, if desired.

SERVES 4

2 bunches of watercress
   (about 7 oz/200 g)

3 tbsp butter

2 onions, chopped

8 oz/225 g potatoes, coarsely
   chopped

5 cups Vegetable Stock (see page
   10) or water

whole nutmeg, for grating (optional)

salt and pepper

$^1/_2$ cup yogurt or sour cream, to
   serve

Cream of Pea Soup

Melt the butter in a saucepan over low heat. Add the onion and cook, stirring occasionally, for 5 minutes, until softened.

Add the peas and pour in the water. Increase the heat to medium and simmer for 3–4 minutes, or until the peas are tender. (Frozen peas will be ready in 10 minutes.)

Add 2½ cups of the milk, season with salt and pepper, and then bring to a boil, stirring continuously.

Remove the pan from the heat and let cool slightly, then pour the soup into a food processor and process to a smooth purée.

Return the soup to the rinsed-out pan and bring back to a boil. If the soup seems too thick, heat the remaining milk in a small saucepan and stir it into the soup. Taste and adjust the seasoning if necessary, and serve.

SERVES 4

4 tbsp butter

1 onion, finely chopped

1 lb/450 g shelled peas

½ cup water

2½–3 cups milk

salt and pepper

Asparagus Soup

Wash and trim the asparagus, discarding the woody part of the stem. Cut the remainder into short lengths, reserving a few tips for garnish. Fine asparagus does not need to be trimmed.

Bring a small saucepan of lightly salted water to a boil, add the asparagus tips, and cook for 5–10 minutes. Drain and set aside.

Put the asparagus in a saucepan with the stock, bring to a boil, cover, and simmer for about 20 minutes, until softened. Drain and reserve the stock.

Melt the butter or margarine in a saucepan. Add the onion and cook over low heat until softened, but only barely colored. Stir in the flour and cook for 1 minute, then gradually whisk in the reserved stock and bring to a boil.

Simmer for 2–3 minutes, until thickened, then stir in the cooked asparagus, coriander, lemon juice, and salt and pepper to taste. Simmer for 10 minutes. Remove from the heat and let cool a little. Transfer to a food processor or blender and process until smooth.

Pour into a clean saucepan, add the milk and reserved asparagus tips, and bring to a boil. Simmer for 2 minutes. Stir in the cream, reheat gently, and serve.

SERVES 6

1 bunch asparagus, about 12 oz/ 350 g, or 2 packs fine asparagus, about $5^1/_2$ oz/150 g each

3 cups Vegetable Stock (see page 10)

$^1/_4$ cup butter or margarine

1 onion, chopped

3 tbsp all-purpose flour

$^1/_4$ tsp ground coriander

1 tbsp lemon juice

2 cups milk

4–6 tbsp heavy or light cream

salt and pepper

Creamy Carrot & Parsnip Soup

Melt the butter in a large saucepan over low heat. Add the onion and cook, stirring, for 3 minutes, until slightly softened. Add the carrots and parsnips, cover the pan, and cook, stirring occasionally, for about 15 minutes, until the vegetables have softened a little. Stir in the ginger, orange zest, and stock. Bring to a boil, then reduce the heat, cover the pan, and simmer for 30–35 minutes, until the vegetables are tender. Remove the soup from the heat and let cool for 10 minutes.

Transfer the soup to a food processor or blender and process until smooth. Return the soup to the rinsed-out pan, stir in the cream, and season well with salt and pepper. Warm through gently over low heat.

Remove from the heat and ladle into warmed bowls. Garnish each bowl with pepper and a sprig of cilantro and serve.

SERVES 4

4 tbsp butter

1 large onion, chopped

1 lb/450 g carrots, chopped

2 large parsnips, chopped

1 tbsp grated fresh ginger

1 tsp grated orange zest

2$^1/_2$ cups Vegetable Stock
   (see page 10)

$^1/_2$ cup light cream

salt and pepper

sprigs of fresh cilantro, to garnish

Roasted Squash & Sweet Potato Soup

Preheat the oven to 375°F/190°C.

Cut the sweet potato, squash, and shallots in half lengthwise, through to the stem end. Scoop the seeds out of the squash. Brush the cut sides with the oil.

Put the vegetables, cut-side down, in a shallow roasting pan. Add the garlic cloves. Roast in the preheated oven for about 40 minutes, until tender and light brown.

When cool, scoop the flesh from the potato and squash halves, and put in a saucepan with the shallots. Remove the garlic peel and add the soft insides to the other vegetables.

Add the stock and a pinch of salt. Bring just to a boil, reduce the heat, and simmer, partially covered, for about 30 minutes, stirring occasionally, until the vegetables are very tender.

Let the soup cool slightly, then transfer to a food processor or blender and process until smooth, working in batches, if necessary. (If using a food processor, strain off the cooking liquid and reserve. Process the soup solids with enough cooking liquid to moisten them, then combine with the remaining liquid.)

Return the soup to the rinsed-out pan and stir in the cream. Season with salt and pepper to taste, then simmer for 5–10 minutes until completely heated through. Ladle into warmed serving bowls, garnish with pepper and snipped chives, and serve.

SERVES 6–8

1 sweet potato, about 12 oz/350 g

1 acorn squash

4 shallots

2 tbsp olive oil

5–6 garlic cloves, unpeeled

3³/₄ cups Chicken Stock
   (see page 11)

¹/₂ cup light cream

salt and pepper

snipped chives, to garnish

Sweet Potato & Bleu Cheese Soup

Melt the butter in a large saucepan over medium heat. Add the onion and leeks and cook, stirring, for about 3 minutes, until slightly softened. Add the sweet potatoes and cook for another 5 minutes, stirring, then pour in the stock, add the parsley and the bay leaf, and season with pepper. Bring to a boil, then reduce the heat, cover the pan, and simmer for about 30 minutes. Remove from the heat and let cool for 10 minutes. Remove and discard the bay leaf.

Transfer half of the soup into a food processor and blend until smooth. Return to the pan with the rest of the soup, stir in the cream, and cook for another 5 minutes. Gradually stir in the crumbled cheese until melted (do not let the soup boil).

Remove from the heat and ladle into warmed bowls. Garnish with finely crumbled cheese and serve with slices of fresh bread.

SERVES 4

4 tbsp butter

1 large onion, chopped

2 leeks, trimmed and sliced

6 oz/175 g sweet potatoes, peeled and diced

$3^{1}/_{2}$ cups Vegetable Stock (see page 10)

1 tbsp chopped fresh parsley

1 bay leaf

$^{2}/_{3}$ cup heavy cream

$5^{1}/_{2}$ oz/150 g bleu cheese, crumbled

pepper

2 tbsp finely crumbled bleu cheese, to garnish

thick slices of fresh bread, to serve

Chilled Red Bell Pepper & Orange Soup

Finely grate the rind of one of the oranges and shred the rind of another with a citrus zester. Set aside. Squeeze the juice from all the oranges.

Heat the olive oil in a saucepan, add the bell peppers and cook over medium heat, stirring occasionally, for 10 minutes. Stir in the grated orange rind and cook for an additional few minutes. Reduce the heat, cover, and simmer gently, stirring occasionally, for 20 minutes.

Remove the pan from the heat, let cool slightly, then transfer the red pepper mixture to a food processor and process to a smooth purée. Add the orange juice and orange flower water and process again until thoroughly combined.

Transfer the soup to a bowl, season with salt and pepper to taste, and let cool completely, then cover with plastic wrap and chill in the refrigerator for 3 hours. Stir well before serving sprinkled with the shredded orange rind and drizzled with extra virgin olive oil, if using.

SERVES 4

5 blood oranges

3 tbsp olive oil

3 lb 5 oz/1.5 kg red bell peppers, seeded and sliced

1½ tbsp orange flower water

salt and pepper

extra virgin olive oil, for drizzling (optional)

Spiced Pumpkin Soup

Heat the oil in a saucepan over medium heat. Add the onion and garlic and cook, stirring, for about 4 minutes, until slightly softened. Add the ginger, chile, cilantro, bay leaf, and pumpkin, and cook for another 3 minutes.

Pour in the stock and bring to a boil. Using a slotted spoon, skim any foam from the surface. Reduce the heat and simmer gently, stirring occasionally, for about 25 minutes, or until the pumpkin is tender. Remove from the heat, take out the bay leaf, and let cool a little.

Transfer the soup to a food processor or blender and process until smooth (you may have to do this in batches). Return the mixture to the rinsed-out pan and season with salt and pepper to taste. Reheat gently, stirring. Remove from the heat, pour into warmed soup bowls, garnish each one with a swirl of cream, and serve.

SERVES 4

2 tbsp olive oil

1 onion, chopped

1 garlic clove, chopped

1 tbsp chopped fresh ginger

1 small red chile, seeded and finely chopped

2 tbsp chopped fresh cilantro

1 bay leaf

2 lb 4 oz/1 kg pumpkin, peeled, seeded, and diced

$2^1/_2$ cups Vegetable Stock (see page 10)

salt and pepper

light cream, to garnish

Winter Warmer Red Lentil Soup

Put the lentils, onion, carrots, celery, parsnip, garlic, stock, and paprika into a large saucepan. Bring to a boil and boil rapidly for 10 minutes. Reduce the heat, cover, and simmer for 20 minutes, or until the lentils and vegetables are tender.

Let the soup cool slightly, then purée in small batches in a food processor or blender. Process until the mixture is smooth.

Return the soup to the rinsed-out pan and heat through thoroughly. Season with pepper to taste.

Ladle the soup into warmed bowls, garnish with snipped chives, and serve.

SERVES 6

1 cup dried red lentils

1 red onion, diced

2 large carrots, sliced

1 celery stalk, sliced

1 parsnip, diced

1 garlic clove, crushed

5 cups Vegetable Stock
  (see page 10)

2 tsp paprika

pepper

1 tbsp snipped fresh chives,
  to garnish

Split Pea & Ham Soup

Rinse the peas under cold running water. Put in a saucepan and cover generously with water. Bring to a boil, boil for 3 minutes, skimming off the foam from the surface, and drain.

Heat the oil in a large saucepan over medium heat. Add the onion and cook for 3–4 minutes, stirring occasionally, until just softened.

Add the carrot and celery and continue cooking for 2 minutes. Add the peas, pour over the stock and water, and stir to combine.

Bring just to a boil and stir the ham into the soup. Add the thyme, marjoram, and bay leaf. Reduce the heat, cover, and cook gently for 1–1½ hours, until the ingredients are very soft. Remove the bay leaf.

Taste and adjust the seasoning, adding salt and pepper to taste. Ladle into warmed soup bowls and serve.

SERVES 6–8

1 lb 2 oz/500 g split green peas

1 tbsp olive oil

1 large onion, finely chopped

1 large carrot, finely chopped

1 celery stalk, finely chopped

4 cups Chicken Stock (see page 11) or Vegetable Stock (see page 10)

4 cups water

8 oz/225 g lean smoked ham, finely diced

¼ tsp dried thyme

¼ tsp dried marjoram

1 bay leaf

salt and pepper

Cream of Chicken Soup

Melt the butter in a large saucepan over medium heat. Add the shallots and cook, stirring, for 3 minutes, until slightly softened. Add the leek and cook for another 5 minutes, stirring. Add the chicken, stock, and herbs, and season with salt and pepper. Bring to a boil, then reduce the heat and simmer for 25 minutes, until the chicken is tender and cooked through. Remove from the heat and let cool for 10 minutes.

Transfer the soup to a food processor or blender and process until smooth (you may need to do this in batches). Return the soup to the rinsed-out pan and warm over low heat for 5 minutes.

Stir in the cream and cook for another 2 minutes, then remove from the heat and ladle into warmed bowls. Garnish with sprigs of thyme and serve immediately.

SERVES 4

3 tbsp butter

4 shallots, chopped

1 leek, sliced

1 lb/450 g skinless chicken breasts, chopped

2^1/$_2$ cups Chicken Stock (see page 11)

1 tbsp chopped fresh parsley

1 tbsp chopped fresh thyme, plus extra sprigs to garnish

^{3}/$_4$ cup heavy cream

salt and pepper

Chicken Noodle Soup

Place the chicken breasts in a large saucepan, add the water, and bring to a simmer. Cook for 25–30 minutes. Skim any foam from the surface, if necessary. Remove the chicken from the stock and keep warm.

Continue to simmer the stock, add the carrots and vermicelli, and cook for 4–5 minutes.

Thinly slice or shred the chicken breasts and place in warmed serving dishes.

Season the soup with salt and pepper to taste and pour over the chicken. Serve immediately, garnished with the tarragon.

SERVES 4–6

2 skinless chicken breasts

5 cups water or Chicken Stock (see page 11)

3 carrots, peeled and cut into $^1/_4$-inch/5-mm slices

3 oz/85 g dried vermicelli (or other small noodles)

salt and pepper

fresh tarragon leaves, to garnish

Chicken & Rice Soup

Put the stock in a large saucepan and add the carrots, celery, and leek. Bring to a boil, reduce the heat to low, and simmer gently, partially covered, for 10 minutes.

Stir in the petit pois, rice, and chicken and continue cooking for an additional 10–15 minutes, or until the vegetables are tender.

Add the chopped tarragon and parsley, then taste and adjust the seasoning, adding salt and pepper as needed.

Ladle the soup into warmed bowls, garnish with parsley, and serve.

SERVES 4

$6^1/_4$ cups Chicken Stock
  (see page 11)
2 small carrots, very thinly sliced
1 celery stalk, finely diced
1 baby leek, halved lengthwise and
  thinly sliced
4 oz/115 g petit pois, thawed
  if frozen
1 cup cooked rice
$5^1/_2$ oz/150 g cooked chicken,
  sliced
2 tsp chopped fresh tarragon
1 tbsp chopped fresh parsley
salt and pepper
sprigs of fresh parsley, to garnish

Beef & Vegetable Soup

Place the pearl barley in a large saucepan. Pour over the stock and add the mixed herbs. Bring to a boil, cover, and simmer gently over low heat for 10 minutes.

Meanwhile, trim any fat from the beef and cut the meat into thin strips.

Skim away any foam that has risen to the top of the stock with a flat ladle.

Add the beef, carrot, leek, onion, and celery to the pan. Bring back to a boil, cover, and simmer for about 1 hour or until the pearl barley, beef, and vegetables are just tender.

Skim away any remaining foam that has risen to the top of the soup with a flat ladle. Blot the surface with absorbent paper towels to remove any fat. Adjust the seasoning according to taste.

Ladle the soup into warmed bowls, garnish with chopped parsley, and serve hot.

SERVES 4

$^1/_3$ cup pearl barley

5 cups Beef Stock (see page 11)

1 tsp dried mixed herbs

8 oz/225 g lean porterhouse steak

1 large carrot, diced

1 leek, shredded

1 onion, chopped

2 celery stalks, sliced

salt and pepper

2 tbsp chopped fresh parsley,
   to garnish

Clam & Corn Chowder

If using fresh clams, wash under cold running water. Discard any with broken shells or any that refuse to close when tapped. Put the clams into a heavy-bottom saucepan with the wine. Cover tightly, set over medium–high heat, and cook for 2–4 minutes, or until they open, shaking the pan occasionally. Discard any that remain closed. Remove the clams from the shells and strain the cooking liquid through a very fine mesh sieve; reserve both. If using canned clams, drain and rinse well.

Melt the butter in a large saucepan over medium–low heat. Add the onion and carrot and cook for 3–4 minutes, stirring frequently, until the onion is softened. Stir in the flour and continue cooking for 2 minutes.

Slowly add about half the stock and stir well, scraping the bottom of the pan to mix in the flour. Pour in the remaining stock and the reserved clam cooking liquid, or the water if using canned clams, and bring just to a boil, stirring.

Add the potatoes, corn, and milk and stir to combine. Reduce the heat and simmer gently, partially covered, for about 20 minutes, stirring occasionally, until all the vegetables are tender.

Chop the clams, if large. Stir in the clams and continue cooking for about 5 minutes until heated through. Taste and adjust the seasoning, if necessary.

Ladle the soup into warmed bowls and sprinkle with parsley.

SERVES 4

1 lb 10 oz/750 g clams, or
   10 oz/280 g canned clams

2 tbsp dry white wine (if using
   fresh clams)

4 tsp butter

1 large onion, finely chopped

1 small carrot, finely diced

3 tbsp all-purpose flour

$1^{1}/_{4}$ cups Fish Stock (see page 10)

$^{3}/_{4}$ cup water (if using
   canned clams)

1 lb/450 g potatoes, diced

1 cup corn, thawed if frozen

2 cups milk

salt and pepper

chopped fresh parsley, to garnish

Hearty Soups

These nourishing and satisfying bowlfuls are the ideal comfort food on a cold winter's day. Try Tuscan Bean Soup or Mushroom & Barley Soup—both are meals in themselves, but if you are feeling particularly hungry, you can serve some chunks of fresh bread alongside. These soups will keep you going, however hectic your day might be.

Vegetable Soup with Pesto

Heat the oil in a large saucepan over medium–low heat. Add the onion and leek and cook for 5 minutes, stirring occasionally, until the onion is softened. Add the celery, carrot, and garlic and cook, covered, for an additional 5 minutes, stirring frequently.

Add the water, potato, parsnip, kohlrabi, and green beans. Bring to a boil, reduce the heat to low, and simmer, covered, for 5 minutes.

Add the peas, zucchini, and cannellini beans, and season generously with salt and pepper. Cover again and simmer for about 25 minutes, until all the vegetables are tender.

Meanwhile, make the pesto. Put the garlic, basil, and Parmesan cheese in a food processor with the oil and process until smooth, scraping down the sides as necessary. Alternatively, pound together using a mortar and pestle.

Add the spinach to the soup and simmer for an additional 5 minutes. Taste and adjust the seasoning and stir about a tablespoon of the pesto into the soup. Ladle into warmed bowls and serve with the remaining pesto.

SERVES 6

1 tbsp olive oil

1 onion, finely chopped

1 large leek, thinly sliced

1 celery stalk, thinly sliced

1 carrot, quartered and thinly sliced

1 garlic clove, finely chopped

$6^1/_4$ cups water

1 potato, diced

1 parsnip, finely diced

1 small kohlrabi or turnip, diced

$5^1/_2$ oz/150 g green beans, cut into small pieces

$5^1/_2$ oz/150 g fresh or frozen peas

2 small zucchini, quartered lengthwise and sliced

14 oz/400 g canned cannellini beans, drained and rinsed

$3^1/_2$ oz/100 g spinach leaves, cut into thin ribbons

salt and pepper

pesto

1 large garlic clove, very finely chopped

$^1/_2$ cup basil leaves

1 cup Parmesan cheese, grated

4 tbsp extra virgin olive oil

Roasted Mediterranean Vegetable Soup

Preheat the oven to 375°F/190°C.

Brush a large shallow baking dish with oil. Laying them cut-side down, arrange the tomatoes, bell peppers, zucchini, and eggplant in one layer (use two dishes, if necessary). Tuck the garlic cloves and onion pieces into the gaps and drizzle the vegetables with the remaining oil. Season lightly with salt and pepper and sprinkle with the thyme.

Place in the preheated oven and bake, uncovered, for 30–35 minutes, or until softened and browned around the edges. Leave to cool, then scrape out the eggplant flesh and remove the skin from the bell peppers.

Working in batches, put the eggplant and bell pepper flesh, together with the tomatoes, zucchini, garlic, and onion, into a food processor and chop to the consistency of salsa; do not purée. Alternatively, place in a bowl and chop together with a knife.

Combine the stock and chopped vegetable mixture in a saucepan and simmer over medium heat for 20–30 minutes, until all the vegetables are tender and the flavors have completely blended.

Stir in the cream and simmer over low heat for about 5 minutes, stirring occasionally, until hot. Taste and adjust the seasoning, if necessary. Ladle the soup into warmed bowls, garnish with basil, and serve.

SERVES 6

3 tbsp olive oil

1 lb 9 oz/700 g ripe tomatoes, peeled, cored, and halved

3 large yellow bell peppers, seeded and halved

3 zucchini, halved lengthwise

1 small eggplant, halved lengthwise

4 garlic cloves, halved

2 onions, cut into eighths

pinch of dried thyme

4 cups Chicken Stock (see page 11), Vegetable Stock (see page 10), or Beef Stock (see page 11)

$^1/_2$ cup light cream

salt and pepper

shredded basil leaves, to garnish

Ribollita

Heat the olive oil in a large saucepan and cook the onions, carrots, and celery for 10–15 minutes, stirring frequently. Add the garlic, thyme, and salt and pepper to taste. Continue to cook for an additional 1–2 minutes, until the vegetables are golden and caramelized.

Add the cannellini beans to the pan and pour in the tomatoes. Add enough of the water to cover the vegetables. Bring to a boil and simmer for 20 minutes. Add the parsley and kale and cook for an additional 5 minutes.

Stir in the bread and add a little more water, if needed. The soup should be thick.

Taste and adjust the seasoning, if necessary. Ladle the soup into warmed serving bowls and serve hot, drizzled with extra virgin olive oil.

SERVES 4

3 tbsp olive oil

2 red onions, coarsely chopped

3 carrots, sliced

3 celery stalks, coarsely chopped

3 garlic cloves, chopped

1 tbsp chopped fresh thyme

14 oz/400 g canned cannellini beans, drained and rinsed

14 oz/400 g canned chopped tomatoes

2^1/$_2$ cups water or Vegetable Stock (see page 10)

2 tbsp chopped fresh parsley

1 lb 2 oz/500 g Tuscan kale or savoy cabbage, trimmed and sliced

1 small day-old ciabatta loaf, torn into small pieces

salt and pepper

extra virgin olive oil, to serve

Vegetable & Corn Chowder

Heat the oil in a large saucepan. Add the onion, bell pepper, garlic, and potato and cook over low heat, stirring frequently, for 2–3 minutes.

Stir in the flour and cook, stirring for 30 seconds. Gradually stir in the milk and stock.

Add the broccoli and corn. Bring the mixture to a boil, stirring continuously, then reduce the heat and simmer for about 20 minutes, or until all the vegetables are tender.

Stir in ½ cup of the cheese until it melts.

Season with salt and pepper to taste and spoon the chowder into warmed serving bowls. Garnish with the remaining cheese and the cilantro and serve.

SERVES 4

1 tbsp vegetable oil

1 red onion, diced

1 red bell pepper, seeded and diced

3 garlic cloves, minced

1 large potato, diced

2 tbsp all-purpose flour

2½ cups milk

1¼ cups Vegetable Stock
   (see page 10)

1¾ oz/50 g broccoli florets

3 cups canned corn, drained

¾ cup cheddar cheese, grated

salt and pepper

1 tbsp chopped fresh cilantro,
   to garnish

Mushroom & Barley Soup

Rinse the pearl barley and drain. Bring 2 cups of the stock to a boil in a small saucepan. Add the bay leaf and, if the stock is unsalted, add a large pinch of salt. Stir in the pearl barley, reduce the heat, cover, and simmer for 40 minutes.

Melt the butter in a large skillet over medium heat. Add the mushrooms and season with salt and pepper. Cook for about 8 minutes until they are golden brown, stirring occasionally at first, then more often after they start to color. Remove the mushrooms from the heat.

Heat the oil in a large saucepan over medium heat and add the onion and carrots. Cover and cook for about 3 minutes, stirring frequently, until the onion is softened.

Add the remaining stock and bring to a boil. Stir in the barley with its cooking liquid and add the mushrooms. Reduce the heat, cover, and simmer gently for about 20 minutes, or until the carrots are tender, stirring occasionally.

Stir in the tarragon and parsley. Taste and adjust the seasoning, if necessary. Ladle into warmed bowls, garnish with fresh parsley and tarragon, and serve.

SERVES 4

$1/3$ cup pearl barley

$6 3/4$ cups Chicken Stock (see page 11) or Vegetable Stock (see page 10)

1 bay leaf

1 tbsp butter

12 oz/350 g mushrooms, thinly sliced

1 tsp olive oil

1 onion, finely chopped

2 carrots, thinly sliced

1 tbsp chopped fresh tarragon, plus extra to garnish

1 tbsp chopped fresh parsley, plus extra to garnish

salt and pepper

Red Kidney Bean, Pumpkin & Tomato Soup

Pick over the beans, cover generously with cold water, and leave to soak for 6 hours or overnight. Drain the beans, put in a saucepan, and add enough cold water to cover by 2 inches/5 cm. Bring to a boil and simmer for 10 minutes. Drain and rinse well.

Heat the oil in a large saucepan over medium heat. Add the onions, cover, and cook for 3–4 minutes, until they are just softened, stirring occasionally. Add the garlic, celery, and carrot, and continue cooking for 2 minutes.

Add the water, drained beans, tomato paste, thyme, oregano, cumin, and bay leaf. When the mixture begins to bubble, reduce the heat to low. Cover and simmer gently for 1 hour, stirring occasionally.

Stir in the tomatoes, pumpkin, and chili paste and continue simmering for an additional hour, or until the beans and pumpkin are tender, stirring from time to time.

Season with salt and pepper to taste and stir in a little more chili paste, if desired. Ladle the soup into warmed bowls, garnish with cilantro, and serve.

SERVES 4–6

9 oz/250 g dried red kidney beans

1 tbsp olive oil

2 onions, finely chopped

4 garlic cloves, finely chopped

1 celery stalk, thinly sliced

1 carrot, halved and thinly sliced

5 cups water

2 tsp tomato paste

$^1/_8$ tsp dried thyme

$^1/_8$ tsp dried oregano

$^1/_8$ tsp ground cumin

1 bay leaf

14 oz/400 g canned chopped tomatoes

9 oz/250 g peeled pumpkin flesh, diced

$^1/_4$ tsp chili paste, or to taste

salt and pepper

fresh cilantro, to garnish

Tuscan Bean Soup

Place half the cannellini beans and half the borlotti beans in a food processor with half the stock and process until smooth. Pour into a large, heavy-bottom saucepan and add the remaining beans. Stir in enough of the remaining stock to achieve the consistency you like, then bring to a boil.

Add the pasta and return to a boil, then reduce the heat and cook for 15 minutes, or until just tender.

Meanwhile, heat 3 tablespoons of the oil in a small skillet. Add the garlic and cook, stirring continuously, for 2–3 minutes, or until golden. Stir the garlic into the soup with the parsley.

Season with salt and pepper to taste and ladle into warmed soup bowls. Drizzle with the remaining olive oil and serve immediately.

SERVES 6

10¹/₂ oz/300 g canned cannellini beans, drained and rinsed

10¹/₂ oz/300 g canned borlotti beans, drained and rinsed

2¹/₂ cups Chicken Stock (see page 11) or Vegetable Stock (see page 10)

4 oz/115 g dried conchigliette or other small pasta shapes

4 tbsp olive oil

2 garlic cloves, very finely chopped

3 tbsp chopped fresh flat-leaf parsley

salt and pepper

Garlic & Chickpea Soup

Heat half the oil in a large, heavy-bottom saucepan. Add the garlic and cook over low heat, stirring frequently, for 2 minutes. Add the chickpeas to the pan with the water, cumin, and ground coriander. Bring to a boil, then reduce the heat and simmer for $2^{1}/_{2}$ hours, or until the chickpeas are tender.

Meanwhile, heat the remaining oil in a separate saucepan. Add the carrots, onions, and celery. Cover and cook over medium–low heat, stirring occasionally, for 20 minutes.

Stir the vegetable mixture into the pan of chickpeas. Transfer about half the soup to a food processor or blender and process until smooth. Return the purée to the pan, add about half the lemon juice, and stir. Taste and add more lemon juice as needed. Season with salt and pepper to taste.

Ladle into warmed soup bowls, sprinkle with the fresh cilantro, and serve.

SERVES 4

$^{1}/_{2}$ cup olive oil

12 garlic cloves, very finely chopped

2 cups dried chickpeas, soaked overnight in cold water and drained

$10^{1}/_{2}$ cups water

1 tsp ground cumin

1 tsp ground coriander

2 carrots, very finely chopped

2 onions, very finely chopped

6 celery stalks, very finely chopped

juice of 1 lemon

salt and pepper

4 tbsp chopped fresh cilantro, to garnish

Corn, Potato & Cheese Soup

Melt the butter in a large, heavy-bottom saucepan. Add the shallots and cook over low heat, stirring occasionally, for 5 minutes, or until softened. Add the potatoes and cook, stirring, for 2 minutes.

Sprinkle in the flour and cook, stirring, for 1 minute. Remove the pan from the heat and stir in the white wine, then gradually stir in the milk. Return the pan to the heat and bring to a boil, stirring continuously, then reduce the heat and simmer.

Stir in the corn kernels, cheese, chopped sage, and cream and heat through gently until the cheese has just melted.

Ladle the soup into warmed bowls, scatter over some croutons, garnish with fresh sage sprigs, and serve.

SERVES 6

2 tbsp butter

2 shallots, finely chopped

8 oz/225 g potatoes, diced

4 tbsp all-purpose flour

2 tbsp dry white wine

1 1/4 cups milk

11 1/2 oz/325 g canned corn kernels, drained

generous 3/4 cup grated Swiss cheese or cheddar cheese

8 10 fresh sage leaves, chopped

generous 1 3/4 cups heavy cream

fresh sage sprigs, to garnish

Croutons (see page 236), to serve

Chunky Potato & Beef Soup

Heat the vegetable oil in a large saucepan. Add the strips of meat to the pan and cook for 3 minutes, turning continuously. Add the potatoes, carrot, celery, and leeks to the pan. Cook for an additional 5 minutes, stirring.

Pour the stock into the pan and bring to a boil. Reduce the heat until the liquid is simmering, then add the baby corn and the bouquet garni. Cook for an additional 20 minutes, or until cooked through.

Remove and discard the bouquet garni. Stir the dry sherry into the soup, then season with salt and pepper to taste.

Ladle the soup into warmed bowls, garnish with chopped parsley, and serve.

SERVES 4

2 tbsp vegetable oil

8 oz/225 g lean braising steak, cut into strips

8 oz/225 g new potatoes, halved

1 carrot, diced

2 celery stalks, sliced

2 leeks, sliced

$3^1/_2$ cups Beef Stock (see page 11)

8 baby corn, sliced

1 bouquet garni

2 tbsp dry sherry

salt and pepper

chopped fresh parsley, to garnish

Beef Consommé with Eggs & Parmesan Cheese

Pour the consommé into a large saucepan and heat gently, stirring occasionally.

Meanwhile, beat the eggs in a bowl until combined, then stir in the breadcrumbs and Parmesan cheese. Season with salt.

As soon as the consommé comes to a boil, add the egg mixture. When it floats to the surface, stir with a fork to break it up. Ladle into warmed soup bowls and serve immediately.

SERVES 4

$6^1/_3$ cups Consommé (see page 210) or Beef Stock (see page 11)

3 eggs

$^1/_2$ cup fresh white breadcrumbs

$^1/_2$ cup freshly grated Parmesan cheese

salt

Cheese & Bacon Soup

Melt the butter in a large saucepan over medium heat. Add the garlic and onion and cook, stirring, for 3 minutes, until slightly softened. Add the chopped bacon and leeks and cook for another 3 minutes, stirring.

In a bowl, mix the flour with enough stock to make a smooth paste and stir it into the pan. Cook, stirring, for 2 minutes. Pour in the remaining stock, then add the potatoes. Season with salt and pepper. Bring the soup to a boil, then reduce the heat and simmer gently for 25 minutes, until the potatoes are tender and cooked through.

Stir in the cream and cook for 5 minutes, then gradually stir in the cheese until melted. Remove from the heat and ladle into warmed serving bowls. Garnish with the grated cheese and serve immediately.

SERVES 4

2 tbsp butter

2 garlic cloves, chopped

1 large onion, sliced

9 oz/250 g smoked lean bacon, chopped

2 large leeks, trimmed and sliced

2 tbsp all-purpose flour

4 cups Vegetable Stock (see page 10)

1 lb/450 g potatoes, chopped

scant $^1/_2$ cup heavy cream

3 cups grated cheddar cheese, plus extra to garnish

salt and pepper

Sausage & Red Cabbage Soup

Heat the oil in a large saucepan. Add the garlic and onion and cook over medium heat, stirring, for 3 minutes, until slightly softened. Add the leek and cook for another 3 minutes, stirring.

In a bowl, mix the cornstarch with enough stock to make a smooth paste, then stir it into the pan. Cook, stirring, for 2 minutes. Stir in the remaining stock, then add the potatoes and sausages. Season with salt and pepper. Bring to a boil, then reduce the heat and simmer for 25 minutes.

Add the red cabbage and black-eyed peas and cook for 10 minutes, then stir in the cream and cook for another 5 minutes. Remove from the heat and ladle into warmed bowls. Garnish with ground paprika and serve immediately.

SERVES 4

2 tbsp olive oil

1 garlic clove, chopped

1 large onion, chopped

1 large leek, sliced

2 tbsp cornstarch

4 cups Vegetable Stock
   (see page 10)

1 lb/450 g potatoes, sliced

7 oz/200 g skinless sausages, sliced

5^1/$_2$ oz/150 g red cabbage, chopped

7 oz/200 g canned black-eyed peas,
   drained

^{1}/$_2$ cup heavy cream

salt and pepper

ground paprika, to garnish

Hearty Winter Broth

Heat the oil in a large, heavy-bottom saucepan and add the pieces of lamb, turning them to seal and brown on both sides. Lift the lamb out of the pan and set aside until ready to use.

Add the onion, carrots, and leeks to the pan and cook gently for about 3 minutes.

Return the lamb to the pan and add the stock, bay leaf, parsley, and pearl barley. Bring the mixture in the pan to a boil, then reduce the heat. Cover and simmer for 1½ –2 hours.

Discard the parsley sprigs. Lift the pieces of lamb from the broth and let them cool slightly. Remove the bones and any fat and chop the meat. Return the lamb to the broth and reheat gently. Season with salt and pepper to taste.

It is advisable to prepare this soup a day ahead, then leave it to cool, cover, and refrigerate overnight. When ready to serve, remove and discard the layer of fat from the surface and reheat the soup gently. Ladle into warmed bowls and serve immediately.

SERVES 4

1 tbsp vegetable oil

1 lb 2 oz/500 g lean neck of lamb

1 large onion, sliced

2 carrots, sliced

2 leeks, sliced

4 cups Vegetable Stock
  (see page 10)

1 bay leaf

sprigs of fresh parsley

2 oz/55 g pearl barley

salt and pepper

Spicy Lamb Soup with Chickpeas & Zucchini

Heat 1 tablespoon of the oil in a large saucepan or cast-iron casserole over medium–high heat. Add the lamb, in batches if necessary to avoid crowding the pan, and cook until evenly browned on all sides, adding a little more oil if needed. Remove the meat with a slotted spoon when browned.

Reduce the heat and add the onion and garlic to the pan. Cook, stirring frequently, for 1–2 minutes.

Add the water and return all the meat to the pan. Bring just to a boil and skim off any foam that rises to the surface. Reduce the heat and stir in the tomatoes, bay leaf, thyme, oregano, cinnamon, cumin, turmeric, and harissa. Simmer for about 1 hour, or until the meat is very tender. Discard the bay leaf.

Stir in the chickpeas, carrot, and potato and simmer for 15 minutes. Add the zucchini and peas and continue simmering for 15–20 minutes, or until all the vegetables are tender.

Adjust the seasoning, adding more harissa, if desired. Ladle the soup into warmed bowls and garnish with sprigs of mint.

SERVES 4–6

1–2 tbsp olive oil

1 lb/450 g lean boneless lamb, such as shoulder or neck fillet, trimmed of fat and cut into $1/2$-inch/1-cm cubes

1 onion, finely chopped

2–3 garlic cloves, crushed

5 cups water

14 oz/400 g canned chopped tomatoes

1 bay leaf

$1/2$ tsp dried thyme

$1/2$ tsp dried oregano

$1/8$ tsp ground cinnamon

$1/2$ tsp ground cumin

$1/4$ tsp ground turmeric

1 tsp harissa, or more to taste

14 oz/400 g canned chickpeas, rinsed and drained

1 carrot, diced

1 potato, diced

1 zucchini, quartered lengthwise and sliced

$3^1/2$ oz/100 g fresh peas or thawed frozen peas

sprigs of fresh mint or cilantro, to garnish

Beef & Bean Soup

Heat the oil in a large saucepan over medium heat. Add the onion and garlic and cook, stirring frequently, for 5 minutes, or until softened. Add the bell pepper and carrots and cook for an additional 5 minutes.

Meanwhile, drain the peas, reserving the liquid from the can. Place two thirds of the peas, reserving the remainder, in a food processor or blender with the liquid from the peas and process until smooth.

Add the ground beef to the pan and cook, stirring continuously to break up any lumps, until well browned. Add the spices and cook, stirring, for 2 minutes. Add the cabbage, tomatoes, stock, and puréed peas and season with salt and pepper to taste. Bring to a boil, then reduce the heat, cover, and let simmer for 15 minutes, or until the vegetables are tender.

Stir in the reserved peas, cover, and simmer for an additional 5 minutes. Ladle the soup into warmed soup bowls and serve.

SERVES 4

2 tbsp vegetable oil

1 large onion, finely chopped

2 garlic cloves, finely chopped

1 green bell pepper, seeded and sliced

2 carrots, sliced

14 oz/400 g canned black-eyed peas

1 cup fresh ground beef

1 tsp each ground cumin, chili powder, and paprika

$1/4$ head of cabbage, sliced

8 oz/225 g tomatoes, peeled and chopped

$2^1/_2$ cups Beef Stock (see page 11)

salt and pepper

Chicken & Potato Soup with Bacon

Melt the butter in a large saucepan over medium heat. Add the garlic and onion and cook, stirring, for 3 minutes, until slightly softened. Add the chopped bacon and leeks and cook for another 3 minutes, stirring.

In a bowl, mix the flour with enough stock to make a smooth paste and stir it into the pan. Cook, stirring, for 2 minutes. Pour in the remaining stock, then add the potatoes and chicken. Season with salt and pepper. Bring to a boil, then reduce the heat and simmer for 25 minutes, until the chicken and potatoes are tender and cooked through.

Stir in the cream and cook for another 2 minutes, then remove from the heat and ladle into warmed bowls. Garnish with the cooked bacon and flat-leaf parsley and serve immediately.

SERVES 4

1 tbsp butter

2 garlic cloves, chopped

1 onion, sliced

9 oz/250 g smoked lean bacon, chopped

2 large leeks, sliced

2 tbsp all-purpose flour

4 cups Chicken Stock (see page 11)

1 lb 12 oz/800 g potatoes, chopped

7 oz/200 g skinless chicken breast, chopped

4 tbsp heavy cream

salt and pepper

cooked bacon and sprigs of fresh flat-leaf parsley, to garnish

Chicken & Pasta Broth

Put the chicken into a large, flameproof casserole dish with the water, celery, carrot, onion, leek, garlic, peppercorns, allspice berries, herbs, and ½ teaspoon of salt. Bring just to a boil over medium heat and skim off the foam that rises to the surface. Reduce the heat, partially cover, and simmer for 2 hours.

Remove the chicken from the casserole dish and let cool. Continue simmering the liquid, uncovered, for 30 minutes. When the chicken is cool enough to handle, remove the meat from the bones and, if necessary, cut into bite-size pieces. Strain the liquid through a sieve and remove as much fat as possible. Discard the vegetables and flavorings. (There should be about 7½ cups of liquid.)

Bring the liquid to a boil in a clean saucepan over medium heat. Add the pasta and reduce the heat so the liquid simmers very gently. Cook for about 10 minutes, or until the pasta is tender but still firm to the bite.

Stir in the chicken. Taste the soup and adjust the seasoning, if necessary. Ladle into warmed bowls, sprinkle with parsley, and serve.

SERVES 4–6

2 lb 12 oz/1.25 kg chicken pieces, such as wings or legs

8 cups water

1 celery stalk, sliced

1 large carrot, sliced

1 onion, sliced

1 leek, sliced

2 garlic cloves, finely chopped

8 peppercorns

4 allspice berries

3–4 fresh parsley stems

2–3 fresh thyme sprigs

1 bay leaf

3 oz/85 g dried farfalline (small pasta bows)

salt and pepper

chopped fresh parsley, to garnish

Chicken Gumbo Soup

Heat the oil in a large, heavy-bottom saucepan over medium–low heat and stir in the flour. Cook for about 15 minutes, stirring occasionally, until the mixture is a rich golden brown.

Add the onion, bell pepper, and celery and continue cooking for about 10 minutes until the onion softens.

Slowly pour in the stock and bring to a boil, stirring well and scraping the bottom of the pan to mix in the flour. Remove the pan from the heat.

Add the tomatoes and garlic. Stir in the okra and rice and season with salt and pepper to taste. Reduce the heat, cover, and simmer for 20 minutes, or until the okra is tender.

Add the chicken and sausage and continue simmering for about 10 minutes. Taste and adjust the seasoning, if necessary, and ladle into warmed bowls to serve.

SERVES 6

2 tbsp olive oil

4 tbsp all-purpose flour

1 onion, finely chopped

1 small green bell pepper, seeded and finely chopped

1 celery stalk, finely chopped

5 cups Chicken Stock (see page 11)

14 oz/400 g canned chopped tomatoes

3 garlic cloves, finely chopped or crushed

$4^{1}/_{2}$ oz/125 g okra, stems removed, cut into $^{1}/_{4}$-inch/5-mm thick slices

4 tbsp white rice

7 oz/200 g cooked chicken, cubed

4 oz/115 g cooked garlic sausage, sliced or cubed

salt and pepper

Turkey & Lentil Soup

Heat the oil in a large saucepan. Add the garlic and onion and cook over medium heat, stirring, for 3 minutes, until slightly softened. Add the mushrooms, bell pepper, and tomatoes, and cook for another 5 minutes, stirring. Pour in the stock and red wine, then add the cauliflower, carrot, and red lentils. Season with salt and pepper to taste. Bring to a boil, then reduce the heat and simmer for 25 minutes, until the vegetables are tender and cooked through.

Add the turkey and zucchini to the pan and cook for 10 minutes. Stir in the shredded basil and cook for another 5 minutes, then remove from the heat and ladle into warmed bowls. Garnish with fresh basil and serve immediately.

SERVES 4

1 tbsp olive oil

1 garlic clove, chopped

1 large onion, chopped

7 oz/200 g button mushrooms, sliced

1 red bell pepper, seeded and chopped

6 tomatoes, peeled, seeded, and chopped

4 cups Chicken Stock (see page 11)

$2/3$ cup red wine

3 oz/85 g cauliflower florets

1 carrot, chopped

1 cup red lentils

12 oz/350 g cooked turkey, chopped

1 zucchini, chopped

1 tbsp shredded fresh basil, plus extra sprigs to garnish

salt and pepper

Seafood Chowder

Discard any mussels with broken shells or any that refuse to close when tapped. Rinse, pull off any beards, and if there are barnacles, scrape them off with a knife under cold running water. Put the mussels in a large, heavy-bottom saucepan. Cover tightly and cook over high heat for about 4 minutes, or until the mussels open, shaking the pan occasionally. Discard any that remain closed. When they are cool enough to handle, remove the mussels from the shells, adding any additional juices to the cooking liquid. Strain the cooking liquid through a cheesecloth-lined sieve and reserve.

Put the flour in a mixing bowl and very slowly whisk in enough of the stock to make a thick paste. Whisk in a little more stock to make a smooth liquid.

Melt the butter in a heavy-bottom saucepan over medium–low heat. Add the onion, cover, and cook for about 5 minutes, stirring frequently, until softened.

Add the remaining fish stock and bring to a boil. Slowly whisk in the flour mixture until well combined and bring back to a boil, whisking continuously. Add the mussel cooking liquid. Season with salt, if needed, and pepper. Reduce the heat and simmer, partially covered, for 15 minutes.

Add the fish and mussels and continue simmering, stirring occasionally, for about 5 minutes, or until the fish is cooked and begins to flake.

Stir in the shrimp and cream. Taste and adjust the seasoning. Simmer for a few minutes longer to heat through. Ladle into warmed bowls, sprinkle with dill, and serve.

SERVES 6

2 lb 4 oz/1 kg live mussels

4 tbsp all-purpose flour

$6^1/_4$ cups Fish Stock (see page 10)

1 tbsp butter

1 large onion, finely chopped

12 oz/350 g skinless whitefish fillets, such as cod or sole

7 oz/200 g cooked or raw peeled shrimp

$1^1/_4$ cups heavy cream

salt and pepper

snipped fresh dill, to garnish

Fish Soup with Cider

Melt the butter in a large saucepan over medium–low heat. Add the leek and shallots and cook for about 5 minutes, stirring frequently, until they start to soften. Add the cider and bring to a boil.

Stir in the stock, potatoes, and bay leaf and bring back to a boil. Reduce the heat, cover, and cook gently for 10 minutes.

Put the flour in a small bowl and very slowly whisk in a few tablespoons of the milk to make a thick paste. Stir in a little more to make a smooth liquid.

Adjust the heat so the soup bubbles gently. Stir in the flour mixture and cook, stirring frequently, for 5 minutes. Add the remaining milk and half the cream. Continue cooking for about 10 minutes until the potatoes are tender.

Chop the sorrel finely and combine with the remaining cream. (If using a food processor, add the sorrel and chop, then add the cream and process briefly.)

Stir the sorrel cream into the soup and add the fish. Continue cooking, stirring occasionally, for about 3 minutes, until the monkfish stiffens or the cod just begins to flake. Taste the soup and adjust the seasoning, if needed. Ladle into warmed bowls and serve.

SERVES 4

2 tsp butter

1 large leek, thinly sliced

2 shallots, finely chopped

$^1/_2$ cup hard cider

$1^1/_4$ cups Fish Stock (see page 10)

9 oz/250 g potatoes, diced

1 bay leaf

4 tbsp all-purpose flour

$^3/_4$ cup milk

$^3/_4$ cup heavy cream

2 oz/55 g fresh sorrel leaves

12 oz/350 g skinless monkfish fillet or cod fillet, cut into 1-inch/2.5-cm pieces

salt and pepper

Spicy Soups

This chapter explores the world of spice, with an exciting selection of internationally inspired dishes. The recipes range in heat from the warming Beef Goulash Soup to the carefully balanced Hot & Sour Soup with Bean Curd, and from the fiery Middle-Eastern Soup with Harissa to the delicately spiced Thai Chicken–Coconut Soup. All are guaranteed to spice up and add excitement to your meals.

Hot & Sour Soup with Bean Curd

Put the lime rind, garlic, and ginger into a large saucepan with the stock and bring to a boil. Reduce the heat and let simmer for 5 minutes. Remove the lime rind, garlic, and ginger with a slotted spoon and discard.

Meanwhile, heat the vegetable oil in a large skillet over high heat, add the bean curd, and cook, turning frequently, until golden. Remove from the skillet and drain on paper towels.

Add the noodles, mushrooms, and chile to the stock and let simmer for 3 minutes.

Add the bean curd, scallions, soy sauce, lime juice, rice wine, and sesame oil and briefly heat through.

Divide the soup among 4 warmed bowls, sprinkle over the cilantro, and serve at once.

SERVES 4

3 strips of rind and juice of 1 lime

2 garlic cloves, peeled

2 slices fresh ginger

4 cups Chicken Stock (see page 11)

1 tbsp vegetable oil

$5^1/_2$ oz/150 g firm bean curd (drained weight), cubed

7 oz/200 g dried fine egg noodles

$3^1/_2$ oz/100 g shiitake mushrooms, sliced

1 fresh red chile, seeded and sliced

4 scallions, sliced

1 tsp soy sauce

1 tsp Chinese rice wine

1 tsp sesame oil

chopped fresh cilantro, to garnish

Mushroom & Ginger Soup

Soak the dried Chinese mushrooms (if using) for at least 30 minutes in 1¼ cups of the hot stock. Drain the mushrooms and reserve the stock. Remove the stems of the mushrooms and discard. Slice the caps and reserve. Cook the noodles for 2–3 minutes in boiling water, then drain and rinse. Reserve until required.

Heat the corn oil in a preheated wok or large, heavy-bottom skillet over high heat. Add the garlic and ginger, stir, and add the mushrooms. Stir over high heat for 2 minutes.

Add the remaining vegetable stock with the reserved mushroom stock and bring to a boil. Add the soy sauce. Stir in the bean sprouts and cook until tender.

Place some noodles in each soup bowl and ladle the soup on top. Garnish with fresh cilantro sprigs and serve immediately.

SERVES 4

½ oz / 15 g dried Chinese
  mushrooms or 4½ oz / 125 g
  portobello or cremini mushrooms
4 cups hot Vegetable Stock
  (see page 10)
4½ oz / 125 g vermicelli noodles
2 tsp corn oil
3 garlic cloves, crushed
1-inch / 2.5-cm piece fresh ginger,
  finely shredded
1 tsp light soy sauce
4½ oz / 125 g bean sprouts
fresh cilantro sprigs, to garnish

Curried Zucchini Soup

Melt the butter in a large saucepan over medium heat. Add the onion and cook for about 3 minutes until it begins to soften.

Add the zucchini, stock, and curry powder, along with a large pinch of salt, if using unsalted stock. Bring the soup to a boil, reduce the heat, cover, and cook gently for about 25 minutes until the vegetables are tender.

Allow the soup to cool slightly, then transfer to a food processor or blender, working in batches if necessary. Process the soup until just smooth, but still with green flecks. (If using a food processor, strain off the cooking liquid and reserve. Process the soup solids with enough cooking liquid to moisten them, then combine with the remaining liquid.)

Return the soup to the rinsed-out pan and stir in the sour cream. Reheat gently over low heat just until hot. (Do not boil.)

Taste and adjust the seasoning, if needed. Ladle into warmed bowls, garnish with a swirl of sour cream, and serve.

SERVES 4

2 tsp butter

1 large onion, finely chopped

2 lb/900 g zucchini, sliced

2 cups Chicken Stock (see page 11) or Vegetable Stock (see page 10)

1 tsp curry powder

$^1/_2$ cup sour cream, plus extra to garnish

salt and pepper

Curried Chicken Soup

Melt the butter in a large saucepan over medium heat, add the onions, and sauté gently, until softened but not browned.

Add the turnip, carrots, and apple and continue to cook for an additional 3–4 minutes.

Stir in the curry powder until the vegetables are well coated, then pour in the stock. Bring to a boil, cover, and simmer for about 45 minutes. Season well with salt and pepper to taste and add the lemon juice.

Transfer the soup to a food processor or blender. Process until smooth and return to the rinsed-out pan. Add the chicken and cilantro to the pan and heat through.

Place a spoonful of rice in each serving bowl and pour the soup over the top. Garnish with cilantro and serve.

SERVES 4–6

$^1/_4$ cup butter

2 onions, chopped

1 small turnip, cut into small dice

2 carrots, finely sliced

1 apple, peeled, cored, and chopped

2 tbsp mild curry powder

5 cups Chicken Stock (see page 11)

juice of $^1/_2$ lemon

6 oz/175 g cold cooked chicken, cut into small pieces

2 tbsp chopped fresh cilantro, plus extra to garnish

salt and pepper

$^1/_2$ cup cooked rice, to serve

Thai Chicken–Coconut Soup

Soak the dried noodles in a large bowl with enough lukewarm water to cover for 20 minutes, until softened. Alternatively, cook according to the package directions. Drain well and set aside.

Meanwhile, bring the stock to a boil in a large saucepan over high heat. Reduce the heat, add the lemongrass, ginger, lime leaves, and chile and simmer for 5 minutes. Add the chicken and continue simmering for an additional 3 minutes, or until cooked. Stir in the coconut cream, nam pla, and lime juice and continue simmering for 3 minutes. Add the bean sprouts and scallions and simmer for an additional 1 minute. Taste and gradually add extra nam pla or lime juice at this point, if needed. Remove and discard the lemongrass stalk.

Divide the noodles among 4 bowls. Bring the soup back to a boil, then ladle into the bowls. The heat of the soup will warm the noodles. To garnish, sprinkle with cilantro leaves.

SERVES 4

4 oz/115 g dried cellophane noodles

5 cups Chicken Stock (see page 11) or Vegetable Stock (see page 10)

1 lemongrass stalk, crushed

$1/2$-inch/1-cm piece fresh ginger, peeled and very finely chopped

2 fresh kaffir lime leaves, thinly sliced

1 fresh red chile, or to taste, seeded and thinly sliced

2 skinless, boneless chicken breasts, thinly sliced

scant 1 cup coconut cream

2 tbsp nam pla (Thai fish sauce)

1 tbsp fresh lime juice

scant $1/2$ cup bean sprouts

4 scallions, green part only, finely sliced

fresh cilantro leaves, to garnish

Duck with Scallion Soup

Slash the skin of the duck 3 or 4 times with a sharp knife and rub in the curry paste. Cook the duck breasts, skin-side down, in a wok or skillet over high heat for 2–3 minutes. Turn over, reduce the heat, and cook for an additional 3–4 minutes, until cooked through. Lift out and slice thickly. Set aside and keep warm.

Meanwhile, heat the oil in a wok or large skillet and stir-fry half the scallions, the garlic, ginger, carrots, and bell pepper for 2–3 minutes. Pour in the stock and add the chili sauce, soy sauce, and mushrooms. Bring to a boil, reduce the heat, and simmer for 4–5 minutes.

Ladle the soup into warmed bowls, top with the duck slices, and garnish with the remaining scallions. Serve immediately.

SERVES 4

2 duck breasts, skin on

2 tbsp red curry paste

2 tbsp vegetable or peanut oil

bunch of scallions, chopped

2 garlic cloves, crushed

2-inch/5-cm piece fresh ginger, grated

2 carrots, thinly sliced

1 red bell pepper, seeded and cut into strips

4 cups Chicken Stock (see page 11)

2 tbsp sweet chili sauce

3–4 tbsp Thai soy sauce

14 oz/400 g canned straw mushrooms, drained

Spicy Beef & Noodle Soup

Pour the stock into a large saucepan and bring to a boil. Meanwhile, heat the oil in a wok or large skillet. Add a third of the noodles and cook for 10–20 seconds, until they have puffed up. Lift out with tongs, drain on paper towels, and set aside. Discard all but 2 tablespoons of the oil.

Add the shallots, garlic, and ginger to the wok and stir-fry for 1 minute. Add the beef and curry paste and stir-fry for an additional 3–4 minutes, until tender.

Add the beef mixture, the uncooked noodles, soy sauce, and fish sauce to the pan of stock and simmer for 2–3 minutes, until the noodles have swelled. Serve hot, garnished with the chopped cilantro and the reserved crispy noodles.

SERVES 4

4 cups Beef Stock (see page 11)

$^2/_3$ cup vegetable or peanut oil

3 oz/85 g rice vermicelli noodles

2 shallots, sliced thinly

2 garlic cloves, crushed

1-inch/2.5-cm piece fresh ginger, thinly sliced

8-oz/225-g piece beef tenderloin, cut into thin strips

2 tbsp Thai green curry paste

2 tbsp Thai soy sauce

1 tbsp fish sauce

chopped fresh cilantro, to garnish

Mexican-Style Beef & Rice Soup

Heat half the oil in a large skillet over medium–high heat. Add the meat in one layer and cook until well browned, turning to color all sides. Remove the skillet from the heat and pour in the wine.

Heat the remaining oil in a large saucepan over medium heat. Add the onion, cover, and cook for about 3 minutes, stirring occasionally, until just softened. Add the bell pepper, chile, garlic, and carrot, and continue cooking, covered, for 3 minutes.

Add the coriander, cumin, cinnamon, oregano, bay leaf, and orange rind. Stir in the tomatoes and stock, along with the beef and wine. Bring almost to a boil and, when the mixture begins to bubble, reduce the heat to low. Cover and simmer gently, stirring occasionally, for about 1 hour, until the meat is tender.

Stir in the rice, raisins, and chocolate, and continue cooking, stirring occasionally, for about 30 minutes, until the rice is tender.

Ladle into warmed bowls and garnish with cilantro.

SERVES 4

3 tbsp olive oil

1 lb 2 oz/500 g boneless braising beef, cut into 1-inch/2.5-cm pieces

$^2/_3$ cup red wine

1 onion, finely chopped

1 green bell pepper, seeded and finely chopped

1 small fresh red chile, seeded and finely chopped

2 garlic cloves, finely chopped

1 carrot, finely chopped

$^1/_4$ tsp ground coriander

$^1/_4$ tsp ground cumin

$^1/_8$ tsp ground cinnamon

$^1/_4$ tsp dried oregano

1 bay leaf

grated rind of $^1/_2$ orange

14 oz/400 g canned chopped tomatoes

5 cups Beef Stock (see page 11)

$^1/_4$ cup long-grain white rice

3 tbsp raisins

$^1/_2$ oz/15 g semisweet chocolate, melted

chopped fresh cilantro, to garnish

Beef Goulash Soup

Heat the oil in a large wide saucepan over medium–high heat. Add the beef and sprinkle with salt and pepper. Cook until lightly browned.

Reduce the heat and add the onions and garlic. Cook for about 3 minutes, stirring frequently, until the onions are softened. Stir in the flour and continue cooking for 1 minute.

Add the water and stir to combine well, scraping the bottom of the pan to mix in the flour. Stir in the tomatoes, carrot, bell pepper, paprika, caraway seeds, oregano, and stock.

Bring just to a boil. Reduce the heat, cover, and simmer gently for about 40 minutes, stirring occasionally, until all the vegetables are tender.

Add the tagliatelle to the soup and simmer for an additional 20 minutes, or until the tagliatelle is cooked.

Taste the soup and adjust the seasoning, if necessary. Ladle into warmed bowls and top each with a tablespoon of sour cream. Garnish with cilantro and serve.

SERVES 6

1 tbsp oil

1 lb 2 oz/500 g fresh lean ground beef

2 onions, finely chopped

2 garlic cloves, finely chopped

2 tbsp all-purpose flour

1 cup water

14 oz/400 g canned chopped tomatoes

1 carrot, finely chopped

8 oz/225 g red bell pepper, roasted, peeled, seeded, and chopped

1 tsp Hungarian paprika

$1/4$ tsp caraway seeds

pinch of dried oregano

4 cups Beef Stock (see page 11)

2 oz/55 g dried tagliatelle, broken into small pieces

salt and pepper

sour cream and sprigs of fresh cilantro, to garnish

Bacon & Lentil Soup

Heat a large, heavy-bottom pan or flameproof casserole. Add the bacon and cook over medium heat, stirring, for 4–5 minutes, or until the fat runs. Add the chopped onion, carrots, celery, turnip, and potato and cook, stirring frequently, for 5 minutes.

Add the lentils and bouquet garni and pour in the water. Bring to a boil, reduce the heat, and simmer for 1 hour, or until the lentils are tender.

Remove and discard the bouquet garni and season the soup with pepper to taste, and with salt if necessary. Remove from the heat, ladle into warmed bowls and serve.

SERVES 4

1 lb/450 g thick, rindless smoked
   bacon strips, diced

1 onion, chopped

2 carrots, sliced

2 celery stalks, chopped

1 turnip, chopped

1 large potato, chopped

generous 2 1/4 cups Puy lentils

1 bouquet garni

4 cups water or Chicken Stock
   (see page 11)

salt and pepper

Chorizo & Red Kidney Bean Soup

Heat the oil in a large saucepan. Add the garlic and onions and cook over medium heat, stirring, for 3 minutes, until slightly softened. Add the bell pepper and cook for another 3 minutes, stirring. In a bowl, mix the cornstarch with enough stock to make a smooth paste and stir it into the pan. Cook, stirring, for 2 minutes. Stir in the remaining stock, then add the potatoes and season with salt and pepper. Bring to a boil, then reduce the heat and simmer for 25 minutes, until the vegetables are tender.

Add the chorizo, zucchini, and kidney beans to the pan. Cook for 10 minutes, then stir in the cream and cook for another 5 minutes. Remove from the heat and ladle into warmed bowls.

SERVES 4

2 tbsp olive oil

2 garlic cloves, chopped

2 red onions, chopped

1 red bell pepper, seeded and chopped

2 tbsp cornstarch

4 cups Vegetable Stock (see page 10)

1 lb/450 g potatoes, peeled, halved, and sliced

5 1/2 oz/150 g chorizo sausage, sliced

2 zucchini, trimmed and sliced

7 oz/200 g canned red kidney beans, drained

1/2 cup heavy cream

salt and pepper

Middle-Eastern Soup with Harissa

Preheat the oven to 400°F/200°C. Prick the eggplants, place on a baking sheet, and bake for 1 hour. When cool, peel and chop.

Heat the oil in a saucepan. Add the lamb and cook until browned. Add the onion, stock, and water. Bring to a boil. Reduce the heat and let simmer for 1 hour.

For the harissa, process the bell peppers, coriander seeds, chiles, garlic, and caraway seeds in a food processor. With the motor running, add enough oil to make a paste. Season with salt, then spoon into a jar. Cover with oil, seal, and chill.

Remove the shanks from the stock, cut off the meat, and chop. Add the sweet potato, cinnamon, and cumin to the stock, bring to a boil, cover, and simmer for 20 minutes. Discard the cinnamon and process the mixture in a food processor with the eggplant. Return to the pan, add the lamb and cilantro, and heat until hot. Serve with the harissa.

SERVES 4

2 eggplants

3 tbsp olive oil

6 lamb shanks

1 small onion, chopped

1³/₄ cups Chicken Stock
   (see page 11)

8 cups water

14 oz/400 g sweet potatoes,
   cut into chunks

2-inch/5-cm piece cinnamon stick

1 tsp ground cumin

2 tbsp chopped fresh cilantro

harissa

2 red bell peppers, roasted, peeled,
   seeded, and chopped

¹/₂ tsp coriander seeds, dry-roasted

1 oz/25 g fresh red chiles, chopped

2 garlic cloves, chopped

2 tsp caraway seeds

olive oil

salt

Asian Lamb Soup

Trim all visible fat from the lamb and thinly slice the meat. Cut the slices into bite-size pieces. Spread the meat in one layer on a plate and sprinkle over the garlic and 1 tablespoon of the soy sauce. Let marinate, covered, for at least 10 minutes or up to 1 hour.

Put the stock in a saucepan with the ginger, lemongrass, remaining soy sauce, and the chili paste. Bring just to a boil, reduce the heat, cover, and simmer for 10–15 minutes.

When ready to serve the soup, drop the tomatoes, scallions, bean sprouts, and cilantro leaves into the stock.

Heat the oil in a skillet and add the lamb with its marinade. Stir-fry the lamb just until it is no longer red and divide among warmed bowls.

Ladle over the hot stock and serve immediately.

SERVES 4

$5^1/_2$ oz/150 g lean tender lamb, such as neck fillet or leg steak

2 garlic cloves, very finely chopped

2 tbsp soy sauce

5 cups Chicken Stock (see page 11)

1 tbsp grated fresh ginger

2-inch/5-cm piece lemongrass, sliced into very thin rounds

$^1/_4$ tsp chili paste, or to taste

6–8 cherry tomatoes, quartered

4 scallions, finely sliced

$1^3/_4$ oz/50 g bean sprouts, snapped in half

2 tbsp cilantro leaves

1 tsp olive oil

Wonton Soup

For the wonton filling, mix together the pork, shrimp, ginger, soy sauce, rice wine, scallion, sugar, pepper, and sesame oil, and stir well until the texture is thick and pasty. Set aside for at least 20 minutes.

To make the wontons, place a teaspoon of the filling at the center of a wrapper. Brush the edges with a little egg white. Bring the opposite points toward each other and press the edges together, creating a flowerlike shape. Repeat with the remaining wrappers and filling.

To make the soup, bring the stock to a boil and add the salt and pepper. Boil the wontons in the stock for about 5 minutes, or until the wrappers begin to wrinkle around the filling.

To serve, put the scallion in individual bowls, then spoon in the wontons and soup, and sprinkle with the cilantro.

SERVES 6–8

8 cups Chicken Stock (see page 11)

2 tsp salt

$1/2$ tsp white pepper

2 tbsp finely chopped scallion

1 tbsp chopped cilantro leaves, to serve

wontons

6 oz/175 g ground pork, not too lean

8 oz/225 g raw shrimp, peeled, deveined, and chopped

$1/2$ tsp finely chopped fresh ginger

1 tbsp light soy sauce

1 tbsp Chinese rice wine

2 tsp finely chopped scallion

pinch of sugar

pinch of white pepper

dash of sesame oil

30 square wonton wrappers

1 egg white, lightly beaten

Pork & Vegetable Broth

Heat the oil in a large saucepan. Add the garlic and scallions and cook over medium heat, stirring, for 3 minutes, until slightly softened. Add the bell pepper and cook for an additional 5 minutes, stirring.

In a bowl, mix the cornstarch with enough of the stock to make a smooth paste and stir it into the pan. Cook, stirring, for 2 minutes. Stir in the remaining stock and the soy sauce and rice wine, then add the pork, lemongrass, chile, and ginger. Season with salt and pepper. Bring to a boil, then reduce the heat and simmer for 25 minutes.

Bring a separate saucepan of water to a boil, add the noodles, and cook for 3 minutes. Remove from the heat, drain, then add the noodles to the soup along with the water chestnuts. Cook for another 2 minutes, then remove from the heat and ladle into warmed bowls.

SERVES 4

1 tbsp chili oil

1 garlic clove, chopped

3 scallions, sliced

1 red bell pepper, seeded and finely sliced

2 tbsp cornstarch

4 cups Vegetable Stock (see page 10)

1 tbsp soy sauce

2 tbsp rice wine or dry sherry

5 1/2 oz/150 g pork tenderloin, sliced

1 tbsp finely chopped lemongrass

1 small red chile, seeded and finely chopped

1 tbsp grated fresh ginger

4 oz/115 g fine egg noodles

7 oz/200 g canned water chestnuts, drained and sliced

salt and pepper

Pork Chili Soup

Heat the oil in a large saucepan over medium–high heat. Add the pork, season with salt and pepper, and cook until no longer pink, stirring frequently. Reduce the heat to medium and add the onion, celery, bell pepper, and garlic. Cover and continue cooking for 5 minutes, stirring occasionally, until the onion is softened.

Add the tomato paste, tomatoes, and the stock. Add the coriander, cumin, oregano, and chili powder. Stir the ingredients in to combine well.

Bring just to a boil, reduce the heat to low, cover, and simmer for 30–40 minutes until all the vegetables are very tender. Taste and adjust the seasoning, adding more chili powder if you like it hotter.

Ladle the chili into warmed bowls and sprinkle with cilantro. Top each serving with a spoonful of sour cream and serve.

SERVES 4

2 tsp olive oil

1 lb 2 oz/500 g fresh lean ground pork

1 onion, finely chopped

1 celery stalk, finely chopped

1 red bell pepper, cored, seeded, and finely chopped

2–3 garlic cloves, finely chopped

3 tbsp tomato paste

14 oz/400 g canned chopped tomatoes

2 cups Chicken Stock (see page 11) or meat stock

$1/8$ tsp ground coriander

$1/8$ tsp ground cumin

$1/4$ tsp dried oregano

1 tsp mild chili powder, or to taste

salt and pepper

fresh cilantro leaves, to garnish

sour cream, to serve

Corn, Chile & Chorizo Soup

Heat the oil in a large, heavy-bottom saucepan. Add the onions and cook over low heat, stirring occasionally, for 5 minutes, or until softened. Stir in the corn, cover, and cook for an additional 3 minutes.

Add the stock, half the milk, the chiles, and garlic and season with salt. Bring to a boil, reduce the heat, then cover and simmer for 15–20 minutes.

Stir in the remaining milk. Set aside about $^3/_4$ cup of the soup solids, draining off as much liquid as possible. Transfer the remaining soup to a food processor or blender and process to a coarse purée.

Return the soup to the pan and stir in the reserved soup solids, the chorizo, lime juice, and cilantro. Reheat to the simmering point, stirring continuously. Ladle into warmed bowls and serve at once.

SERVES 4

1 tbsp corn oil

2 onions, chopped

1 lb 4 oz/550 g frozen corn kernels, thawed

$2^1/_2$ cups Chicken Stock (see page 11)

scant 2 cups milk

4 chipotle chiles, seeded and finely chopped

2 garlic cloves, finely chopped

2 oz/55 g thinly sliced chorizo sausage

2 tbsp lime juice

2 tbsp chopped fresh cilantro

salt

Shrimp Laksa

Shell and devein the shrimp. Put the fish stock, salt, and the shrimp heads, shells, and tails in a saucepan over high heat and slowly bring to a boil. Reduce the heat and simmer for 10 minutes.

Meanwhile, make the laksa paste. Put all the ingredients except the oil in a food processor and blend. With the motor running, slowly add up to 2 tablespoons of oil just until a paste forms. (If your food processor is too large to work efficiently with this small quantity, use a mortar and pestle, or make double the quantity and keep leftovers tightly covered in the refrigerator to use another time.)

Heat the oil in a large saucepan over high heat. Add the paste and stir-fry until it is fragrant. Strain the stock through a sieve lined with cheesecloth. Stir the stock into the laksa paste, along with the coconut milk, nam pla, and lime juice. Bring to a boil, then reduce the heat, cover, and simmer for 30 minutes.

Meanwhile, soak the noodles in a large bowl with enough lukewarm water to cover for 20 minutes, until softened. Alternatively, cook according to the package directions. Drain and set aside.

Add the shrimp and bean sprouts to the soup and continue simmering just until the shrimp turn opaque and curl. Divide the noodles among 4 bowls and ladle the soup over, making sure everyone gets an equal share of the shrimp. Garnish with the cilantro and serve.

SERVES 4

20–24 large raw unshelled shrimp

2 cups Fish Stock (see page 10)

pinch of salt

1 tsp peanut oil

2 cups coconut milk

2 tsp nam pla (Thai fish sauce)

$^1/_2$ tbsp lime juice

4 oz/115 g dried medium rice
noodles

$^3/_8$ cup bean sprouts

sprigs of fresh cilantro, to garnish

laksa paste

6 fresh cilantro stalks with leaves

3 large garlic cloves, crushed

1 fresh red chile, seeded and
chopped

1 lemongrass stalk, center part only,
chopped

1-inch/2.5-cm piece fresh ginger,
peeled and chopped

$1^1/_2$ tbsp shrimp paste

$^1/_2$ tsp ground turmeric

2 tbsp peanut oil

Thai-Style Seafood Soup

Put the stock in a saucepan with the lemongrass, lime rind, ginger, and chili paste. Bring just to a boil, reduce the heat, cover, and simmer for 10–15 minutes.

Cut the shrimp almost in half lengthwise, keeping the tail intact.

Strain the stock, return to the pan, and bring to a simmer. Add the scallions and cook for 2–3 minutes. Taste and season with salt, if needed, and stir in a little more chili paste, if desired.

Add the scallops and shrimp and poach for about 1 minute until the scallops turn opaque and the shrimp curl.

Stir in the fresh cilantro leaves, ladle the soup into warmed bowls, dividing the shellfish evenly among them, and garnish with chiles.

SERVES 4

5 cups Fish Stock (see page 10)

1 lemongrass stalk, split lengthwise

pared rind of $\frac{1}{2}$ lime, or 1 lime leaf

1-inch/2.5-cm piece fresh ginger, sliced

$\frac{1}{4}$ tsp chili paste, or to taste

7 oz/200 g large or medium raw shrimp, peeled

4–6 scallions, sliced

9 oz/250 g scallops

2 tbsp fresh cilantro leaves

salt

finely sliced red chiles, to garnish

Corn & Crab Soup

Heat the oil in a large skillet and sauté the garlic, shallots, lemongrass, and ginger over low heat, stirring occasionally, for 2–3 minutes, until softened. Add the stock and coconut milk and bring to a boil. Add the corn, reduce the heat, and simmer gently for 3–4 minutes.

Add the crabmeat, fish sauce, lime juice, and sugar, and simmer gently for 1 minute. Ladle into warmed bowls, garnish with the chopped cilantro, and serve immediately.

SERVES 6

2 tbsp vegetable or peanut oil

4 garlic cloves, finely chopped

5 shallots, finely chopped

2 lemongrass stalks, finely chopped

1-inch/2.5-cm piece fresh ginger, finely chopped

4 cups Chicken Stock (see page 11)

14 oz/400 g canned coconut milk

1 1/2 cups frozen corn kernels

12 oz/350 g canned crabmeat, drained and shredded

2 tbsp fish sauce

juice of 1 lime

1 tsp jaggery or light brown sugar

bunch of fresh cilantro, chopped, to garnish

Light & Refreshing Soups

The recipes in this section are light in texture and fresh in taste, making them perfect for the summer months or as an elegant appetizer. Try Chilled Avocado Soup on a hot day, or Parsnip Soup with Ginger & Orange when it's a little cooler. Remember that the fresher the ingredients, the fuller the flavor of the soup, so make sure you use fresh seasonal produce for the best results.

Golden Vegetable Soup with Green Lentils

Heat the oil in a large saucepan over medium heat, add the onion, garlic, and carrot, and cook for 3–4 minutes, stirring frequently, until the onion starts to soften. Add the cabbage and cook for an additional 2 minutes.

Add the tomatoes, thyme, and 1 bay leaf, then pour in the stock. Bring to a boil, reduce the heat to low, and cook gently, partially covered, for about 45 minutes until the vegetables are tender.

Meanwhile, put the lentils in another saucepan with the remaining bay leaf and the water. Bring just to a boil, reduce the heat, and simmer for about 25 minutes until tender. Drain off any remaining water, and set aside.

When the vegetable soup is cooked, allow it to cool slightly, then transfer to a food processor or blender and process until smooth, working in batches, if necessary. (If using a food processor, strain off the cooking liquid and reserve. Purée the soup solids with enough cooking liquid to moisten them, then combine with the remaining liquid.)

Return the soup to the pan and add the cooked lentils. Taste and add salt and pepper to taste, and cook for about 10 minutes to heat through. Ladle into warmed bowls and garnish with parsley.

SERVES 6

1 tbsp olive oil

1 onion, finely chopped

1 garlic clove, finely chopped

1 carrot, halved and thinly sliced

1 lb/450 g green cabbage, cored, quartered, and thinly sliced

14 oz/400 g canned chopped tomatoes

$^1/_2$ tsp dried thyme

2 bay leaves

$6^1/_4$ cups Chicken Stock (see page 11) or Vegetable Stock (see page 10)

7 oz/200 g French green lentils

2 cups water

salt and pepper

chopped fresh parsley, to garnish

Sweet & Sour Cabbage Soup

Put the golden raisins in a bowl, pour over the orange juice, and set aside for 15 minutes.

Heat the oil in a large saucepan over medium heat, add the onion, cover, and cook for 3–4 minutes, stirring frequently, until it starts to soften. Add the cabbage and cook for an additional 2 minutes; do not let it brown.

Add the apples and apple juice, cover, and cook gently for 5 minutes.

Stir in the tomatoes, tomato juice, pineapple, and water. Season with salt and pepper and add the vinegar. Add the golden raisins together with the orange juice soaking liquid. Bring to a boil, reduce the heat, and simmer, partially covered, for about 1 hour, until the fruit and vegetables are tender.

Let the soup cool slightly, then transfer to a food processor or blender and process until smooth, working in batches if necessary. (If using a food processor, strain off the cooking liquid and reserve. Purée the soup solids with enough cooking liquid to moisten them, then combine with the remaining liquid.)

Return the soup to the rinsed-out pan and simmer gently for about 10 minutes to reheat. Ladle into warmed bowls. Garnish with mint leaves and serve immediately.

SERVES 4–6

$^1/_2$ cup golden raisins

$^1/_2$ cup orange juice

1 tbsp olive oil

1 large onion, chopped

3 cups shredded cabbage

2 apples, peeled and diced

$^1/_2$ cup apple juice

14 oz/400 g canned peeled tomatoes

1 cup tomato juice or vegetable juice

$3^1/_2$ oz/100 g pineapple, finely chopped

5 cups water

2 tsp wine vinegar

salt and pepper

fresh mint leaves, to garnish

Parsnip Soup with Ginger & Orange

Heat the olive oil in a large saucepan over medium heat. Add the onion and leek and cook for about 5 minutes, stirring occasionally, until softened.

Add the carrots, parsnips, ginger, garlic, grated orange rind, water, and a large pinch of salt. Reduce the heat, cover, and simmer for about 40 minutes, stirring occasionally, until the vegetables are very soft.

Allow the soup to cool slightly, then transfer to a food processor or blender and process until smooth, working in batches if necessary. (If using a food processor, strain off the cooking liquid and reserve. Purée the soup solids with enough cooking liquid to moisten them, then combine with the remaining liquid.)

Return the soup to the rinsed-out pan and stir in the orange juice. Add a little water or more orange juice, if you prefer a thinner consistency. Taste and adjust the seasoning if necessary. Simmer for about 10 minutes to heat through.

Ladle into warmed bowls, garnish with chives, and serve.

SERVES 6

2 tsp olive oil

1 large onion, chopped

1 large leek, sliced

2 carrots, thinly sliced

1 lb 12 oz/800 g parsnips, sliced

4 tbsp grated fresh ginger

2–3 garlic cloves, finely chopped

grated rind of $^1/_2$ orange

6 cups water

1 cup orange juice

salt and pepper

snipped chives, to garnish

Carrot, Apple & Celery Soup

Place the carrots, onion, and celery in a large saucepan and add the stock. Bring to a boil, reduce the heat, cover, and let simmer for 10 minutes.

Meanwhile, peel, core, and dice 2 of the apples. Add the diced apple, tomato paste, bay leaf, and sugar to the pan and bring to a boil over medium heat. Reduce the heat, partially cover, and let simmer for 20 minutes. Remove and discard the bay leaf.

Meanwhile, wash and core the remaining apple and cut into thin slices, without peeling. Place the apple slices in a small saucepan and squeeze over the lemon juice. Heat the apple slices gently and let simmer for 1–2 minutes, or until the apple is tender. Drain the apple slices and set aside until ready to use.

Place the carrot and apple mixture in a food processor or blender and process until smooth. Return the soup to the rinsed-out pan, reheat gently, if necessary, and season with salt and pepper to taste. Ladle the soup into 4 warmed bowls, top with the reserved apple slices and shredded celery leaves, and serve immediately.

SERVES 4

2 lb/900 g carrots, finely diced

1 medium onion, chopped

3 celery stalks, diced

4 cups Vegetable Stock
  (see page 10)

3 apples

2 tbsp tomato paste

1 bay leaf

2 tsp superfine sugar

$1/4$ large lemon

salt and pepper

shredded celery leaves, to garnish

Beans & Greens Soup

Pick over the beans, cover generously with cold water, and let soak for 6 hours or overnight. Drain the beans, put in a saucepan, and add enough cold water to cover by 2 inches/5 cm. Bring to a boil and boil for 10 minutes. Drain and rinse well.

Heat the oil in a large saucepan over medium heat. Add the onions and cook, covered, for 3–4 minutes, stirring occasionally, until the onions are just softened. Add the garlic, celery, and carrots, and continue cooking for 2 minutes.

Add the water, drained beans, thyme, marjoram, and bay leaf. When the mixture begins to bubble, reduce the heat to low. Cover and simmer gently, stirring occasionally, for about 1¼ hours until the beans are tender. Season with salt and pepper.

Let the soup cool slightly, then transfer 2 cups to a food processor or blender. Process until smooth and recombine with the soup.

A handful at a time, cut the greens crosswise into thin ribbons, keeping tender leaves like spinach separate. Add the thicker leaves and cook gently, uncovered, for 10 minutes. Stir in any remaining greens and continue cooking for 5–10 minutes, until all the greens are tender.

Taste and adjust the seasoning, if necessary. Ladle the soup into warmed bowls and serve.

SERVES 4

9 oz/250 g dried cannellini beans

1 tbsp olive oil

2 onions, finely chopped

4 garlic cloves, finely chopped

1 celery stalk, thinly sliced

2 carrots, halved and thinly sliced

5 cups water

$1/4$ tsp dried thyme

$1/4$ tsp dried marjoram

1 bay leaf

$4^1/2$ oz/125 g leafy greens, such as chard, mustard, spinach, and kale,

salt and pepper

Minted Pea & Yogurt Soup

Heat the oil in a saucepan, add the onions and potato, and cook over low heat, stirring occasionally, for about 3 minutes, until the onion is softened and translucent.

Stir in the garlic, ginger, coriander, cumin, and flour and cook, stirring continuously, for 1 minute.

Add the stock, peas, and the chopped mint and bring to a boil, stirring. Reduce the heat, cover, and simmer gently for 15 minutes, or until the vegetables are tender.

Process the soup, in batches, in a food processor or blender. Return the mixture to the pan and season with salt and pepper to taste. Blend the yogurt with the cornstarch to a smooth paste and stir into the soup. Add the milk and bring almost to a boil, stirring continuously. Cook very gently for 2 minutes.

Serve the soup hot, garnished with the mint sprigs and a swirl of yogurt.

SERVES 6

2 tbsp vegetable or sunflower oil

2 onions, coarsely chopped

8 oz/225 g potatoes, coarsely chopped

2 garlic cloves, minced

1-inch/2.5-cm piece fresh ginger, chopped

1 tsp ground coriander

1 tsp ground cumin

1 tbsp all-purpose flour

$3^1/_2$ cups Vegetable Stock (see page 10)

1 lb 2 oz/500 g frozen peas

2–3 tbsp chopped fresh mint, plus extra sprigs to garnish

$^2/_3$ cup Greek-style yogurt, plus extra to serve

$^1/_2$ tsp cornstarch

$1^1/_4$ cups milk

salt and pepper

Spinach Soup

Heat the oil in a heavy-bottom saucepan over medium heat. Add the onion and leek and cook for about 3 minutes, stirring occasionally, until they begin to soften.

Add the potato, water, marjoram, thyme, and bay leaf, along with a large pinch of salt. Bring to a boil, reduce the heat, cover, and cook gently for about 25 minutes until the vegetables are tender. Remove the bay leaf and the herb stems.

Add the spinach and continue cooking for 3–4 minutes, stirring frequently, just until it is completely wilted.

Let the soup cool slightly, then transfer to a food processor or blender and process until smooth, working in batches if necessary. (If using a food processor, strain off the cooking liquid and reserve. Purée the soup solids with enough cooking liquid to moisten them, then combine with the remaining liquid.)

Return the soup to the rinsed-out pan and thin with a little more water, if desired. Season with salt, a good grinding of pepper, and a generous grating of nutmeg. Place over low heat and simmer until reheated.

Ladle the soup into warmed bowls and swirl a tablespoonful of cream into each serving.

SERVES 4

1 tbsp olive oil

1 onion, halved and thinly sliced

1 leek, split lengthwise and thinly sliced

1 potato, finely diced

4 cups water

2 sprigs fresh marjoram or $^1/_4$ tsp dried

2 sprigs fresh thyme or $^1/_4$ tsp dried

1 bay leaf

14 oz/400 g young spinach

freshly grated nutmeg

salt and pepper

4 tbsp light cream, to serve

Miso Soup

Put the water in a large saucepan with the dashi granules and bring to a boil. Add the bean curd and mushrooms, reduce the heat, and simmer for 3 minutes.

Stir in the miso paste and simmer gently, stirring, until it has dissolved.

Add the scallions and serve immediately. If you leave the soup, the miso will settle, so give the soup a thorough stir before serving to recombine.

SERVES 4

4 cups water

2 tsp dashi granules

6 oz/175 g silken bean curd, drained and cut into small cubes

4 shiitake mushrooms, finely sliced

4 tbsp miso paste

2 scallions, chopped

Gazpacho

Tear the bread into pieces and place in a blender. Process briefly to make breadcrumbs and transfer to a large bowl. Add the tomatoes, garlic, bell peppers, cucumber, oil, vinegar, and tomato paste. Mix well.

Working in batches, place the tomato mixture with about the same amount of the measured water in the food processor or blender and process to a purée. Transfer to another bowl. When all the tomato mixture and water have been blended together, stir well and season with salt and pepper to taste. Cover with plastic wrap and chill in the refrigerator for at least 2 hours, but no longer than 12 hours.

When ready to serve, pour the soup into chilled serving bowls and float an ice cube in each bowl.

SERVES 4

9 oz/250 g white bread slices, crusts removed

1 lb 9 oz/700 g tomatoes, peeled and chopped

3 garlic cloves, coarsely chopped

2 red bell peppers, seeded and chopped

1 cucumber, peeled, seeded, and chopped

5 tbsp extra virgin olive oil

5 tbsp red wine vinegar

1 tbsp tomato paste

9^1/$_2$ cups water

salt and pepper

4 ice cubes, to serve

Chilled Avocado Soup

Put the lemon juice into a food processor or blender. Halve the avocados and remove the pits. Scoop out the flesh and chop coarsely.

Place the avocado flesh, chives, parsley, stock, cream, and Worcestershire sauce in the food processor and process to a smooth purée.

Transfer to a bowl and season with salt and pepper to taste. Cover the bowl tightly with plastic wrap and chill in the refrigerator for at least 30 minutes.

To serve, stir, then ladle into chilled soup bowls and garnish with a swirl of cream and a sprinkling of snipped chives.

SERVES 4

1 tbsp lemon juice

2 avocados

1 tbsp snipped fresh chives, plus extra to garnish

1 tbsp chopped fresh flat-leaf parsley

scant 2 cups cold Chicken Stock (see page 11)

$1^1/_4$ cups light cream, plus extra to garnish

dash of Worcestershire sauce

salt and pepper

Chilled Borscht

Place the cabbage in a saucepan and cover generously with cold water. Bring to a boil, boil for 3 minutes, then drain.

Heat the oil in a large saucepan over medium–low heat. Add the onion and leek, cover, and cook for about 5 minutes, stirring occasionally, until the vegetables begin to soften.

Add the tomatoes, water, carrot, parsnip, beets, and bay leaf. Stir in the blanched cabbage and add a large pinch of salt. Bring to a boil, reduce the heat, and simmer for about 1¼ hours, until all the vegetables are tender. Remove and discard the bay leaf.

Let the soup cool slightly, then transfer to a food processor or blender and process until smooth, working in batches if necessary. (If using a food processor, strain off the cooking liquid and reserve. Purée the soup solids with enough cooking liquid to moisten them, then combine with the remaining liquid.)

Scrape the soup into a large container and stir in the tomato juice. Let cool and refrigerate until cold.

Add the dill and stir. Thin the soup with more tomato juice or water, if desired. Season with salt and pepper to taste and, if you prefer it less sweet, add a few drops of lemon juice. Ladle into chilled soup bowls and top each with a spoonful of sour cream and a sprig of dill.

SERVES 4–6

¼ head of cabbage, cored and coarsely chopped

1 tbsp vegetable oil

1 onion, finely chopped

1 leek, halved lengthwise and sliced

14 oz/400 g canned peeled tomatoes

5 cups water, plus extra if needed

1 carrot, thinly sliced

1 small parsnip, finely chopped

3 beets (raw or cooked), peeled and cubed

1 bay leaf

1½ cups tomato juice, plus extra if needed

2–3 tbsp chopped fresh dill, plus extra sprigs to garnish

fresh lemon juice (optional)

salt and pepper

sour cream or yogurt, to garnish

Asian Duck Broth

Put the duck in a large saucepan with the water. Bring just to a boil and skim off the foam that rises to the surface. Add the stock, ginger, carrot, onion, leek, garlic, peppercorns, and soy sauce. Reduce the heat and simmer, partially covered, for 1½ hours.

Remove the duck from the stock and set aside. When the duck is cool enough to handle, remove the meat from the bones and slice thinly or shred into bite-size pieces, discarding any fat.

Strain the stock, pressing with the back of a spoon to extract all the liquid. Remove as much fat as possible. Discard the vegetables and herbs.

Bring the stock just to a boil in a clean saucepan and add the strips of carrot and leek, the mushrooms, and duck meat. Reduce the heat and cook gently for 5 minutes, or until the carrot is just tender.

Stir in the watercress and continue simmering for 1–2 minutes until it is wilted. Taste the soup and adjust the seasoning if needed, adding a little more soy sauce, if desired. Ladle the soup into warmed bowls and serve immediately.

SERVES 4–6

2 duck leg quarters, skinned

4 cups water

2½ cups Chicken Stock (see page 11)

1-inch/2.5-cm piece fresh ginger

1 large carrot, sliced

1 onion, sliced

1 leek, sliced

3 garlic cloves, crushed

1 tsp black peppercorns

2 tbsp soy sauce, or to taste

1 small carrot, cut into thin strips or slivers

1 small leek, cut into thin strips or slivers

3½ oz/100 g shiitake mushrooms, thinly sliced

1 oz/25 g watercress leaves

salt and pepper

Beef Broth with Herbs & Vegetables

Preheat the oven to 375°F/190°C. To make the stock, trim as much fat as possible from the beef and put in a large roasting pan with the bones and onions. Roast for 30–40 minutes until browned, turning once or twice. Transfer the ingredients to a large flameproof casserole and discard the fat.

Add the water (it should cover by at least 2 inches/5 cm) and bring to a boil. Skim off any foam that rises to the surface. Reduce the heat and add the garlic, carrots, leek, celery, bay leaf, thyme, and a pinch of salt. Simmer very gently, uncovered, for 4 hours, skimming occasionally. Do not stir. If the ingredients emerge from the liquid, top up with water.

Gently ladle the stock through a cheesecloth-lined sieve into a large container and remove as much fat as possible. Save the meat for another purpose, if desired, and discard the bones and vegetables. (There should be about 8 cups of stock.)

Boil the stock very gently until it is reduced to 6¼ cups, or if the stock already has concentrated flavor, measure out that amount and save the rest for another purpose. Taste the stock and adjust the seasoning if necessary.

Bring a saucepan of lightly salted water to a boil and add the celery root and carrots. Reduce the heat, cover, and boil gently for about 15 minutes until tender. Drain.

Add the marjoram and parsley to the boiling stock. Divide the cooked vegetables and diced tomatoes among warmed bowls, ladle over the boiling stock, and serve.

SERVES 4–6

7 oz/200 g celery root, peeled and finely diced

2 large carrots, finely diced

2 tsp chopped fresh marjoram leaves

2 tsp chopped fresh parsley

2 plum tomatoes, peeled, seeded, and diced

rich beef stock

1 lb 4 oz boneless beef shin or braising beef, cut into large cubes

1 lb 10 oz/750 g veal, beef, or pork bones

2 onions, quartered

10 cups water

4 garlic cloves, sliced

2 carrots, sliced

1 large leek, sliced

1 celery stalk, cut into 2-inch/5-cm pieces

1 bay leaf

4–5 sprigs of fresh thyme, or ¼ tsp dried thyme

salt

Fennel & Tomato Soup with Shrimp

Heat the oil in a large saucepan over medium heat. Add the onion and fennel and cook for 3–4 minutes, stirring occasionally, until the onion is just softened.

Add the potato, water, tomato juice, and bay leaf with a large pinch of salt. Reduce the heat, cover, and simmer for about 25 minutes, stirring once or twice, until the vegetables are softened.

Allow the soup to cool slightly, then transfer to a food processor or blender and process until smooth, working in batches if necessary. (If using a food processor, strain off the cooking liquid and reserve. Purée the soup solids with enough cooking liquid to moisten them, then combine with the remaining liquid.)

Return the soup to the saucepan and add the shrimp. Simmer gently for about 10 minutes, to reheat the soup and let it absorb the shrimp flavor.

Stir in the tomatoes and dill. Taste and adjust the seasoning, adding salt, if needed, and pepper. Thin the soup with a little more tomato juice, if desired. Ladle into warmed bowls, garnish with dill or fennel fronds, and serve.

SERVES 4

2 tsp olive oil

1 large onion, halved and sliced

2 large fennel bulbs, halved and sliced

1 small potato, diced

$3^3/4$ cups water

$1^2/3$ cups tomato juice, plus extra if needed

1 bay leaf

$4^1/2$ oz/125 g cooked peeled small shrimp

2 tomatoes, peeled, seeded, and chopped

$^1/2$ tsp snipped fresh dill

salt and pepper

dill sprigs or fennel fronds, to garnish

Salmon & Leek Soup

Heat the oil in a heavy-bottom saucepan over medium heat. Add the onion and leeks and cook for about 3 minutes, until they begin to soften.

Add the potato, stock, water, and bay leaf with a large pinch of salt. Bring to a boil, reduce the heat, cover, and cook gently for about 25 minutes, until the vegetables are tender. Remove the bay leaf.

Let the soup cool slightly, then transfer about half of it to a food processor or blender and process until smooth. (If using a food processor, strain off the cooking liquid and reserve. Purée half the soup solids with enough cooking liquid to moisten them, then combine with the remaining liquid.)

Return the puréed soup to the pan and stir to blend. Reheat gently over medium–low heat.

Season the salmon with salt and pepper and add to the soup. Continue cooking for about 5 minutes, stirring occasionally, until the fish is tender and starts to break up. Stir in the cream, taste, and adjust the seasoning, adding a little lemon juice, if using. Ladle into warmed bowls, garnish with chervil or parsley, and serve.

SERVES 4

1 tbsp olive oil

1 large onion, finely chopped

3 large leeks, including green parts, thinly sliced

1 potato, finely diced

2 cups Fish Stock (see page 10)

3 cups water

1 bay leaf

$10^1/_2$ oz/300 g skinless salmon fillet, cut into $^1/_2$-inch/1-cm cubes

$^1/_3$ cup heavy cream

fresh lemon juice (optional)

salt and pepper

sprigs of fresh chervil or parsley, to garnish

Genoese Fish Soup

Melt the butter in a large, heavy-bottom saucepan. Add the onion and garlic and cook over low heat, stirring occasionally, for 5 minutes, or until softened.

Add the bacon and celery and cook, stirring frequently, for an additional 2 minutes.

Add the tomatoes, wine, stock, basil, and 1 tablespoon of the parsley. Season with salt and pepper to taste. Bring to a boil, then reduce the heat and simmer for 10 minutes.

Add the fish and cook for 5 minutes, or until it is opaque. Add the shrimp and heat through gently for 3 minutes. Ladle into warmed serving bowls, garnish with the remaining chopped parsley, and serve immediately.

SERVES 4

2 tbsp butter

1 onion, chopped

1 garlic clove, finely chopped

2 oz/55 g rindless bacon, diced

2 celery stalks, chopped

14 oz/400 g canned chopped tomatoes

$^2/_3$ cup dry white wine

$1^1/_4$ cups Fish Stock (see page 10)

4 fresh basil leaves, torn

2 tbsp chopped fresh flat-leaf parsley

1 lb/450 g whitefish fillets, such as cod or monkfish, skinned and chopped

4 oz/115 g cooked peeled shrimp

salt and pepper

Luxury Soups

This section includes a range of decadent dishes for those times when you want to impress your friends or just want to indulge yourself. Mushroom & Sherry Soup and Lobster Bisque are sure to hit the spot, and why not give Cold Cucumber & Smoked Salmon Soup or Creamy Oyster Soup a try? These special soups are well worth experimenting with, to the delight of your family and friends.

Mushroom & Sherry Soup

Melt the butter in a large saucepan over low heat. Add the garlic and onions and cook, stirring, for 3 minutes, until slightly softened. Add the mushrooms and cook for another 5 minutes, stirring. Add the chopped parsley, pour in the stock, and season with salt and pepper. Bring to a boil, then reduce the heat, cover the pan, and simmer for 20 minutes.

Put the flour into a bowl, mix in enough milk to make a smooth paste, then stir it into the soup. Cook, stirring, for 5 minutes. Stir in the remaining milk and the sherry and cook for another 5 minutes. Remove from the heat and stir in the sour cream. Return the pan to the heat and warm gently.

Remove from the heat and ladle into warmed bowls. Garnish with chopped fresh parsley and serve immediately.

SERVES 4

4 tbsp butter

2 garlic cloves, chopped

3 onions, sliced

1 lb/450 g mixed button and
   cremini mushrooms, sliced

$3^{1}/_{2}$ oz/100 g fresh porcini
   mushrooms, sliced

3 tbsp chopped fresh parsley, plus
   extra to garnish

2 cups Vegetable Stock
   (see page 10)

3 tbsp all-purpose flour

$^{1}/_{2}$ cup milk

2 tbsp sherry

$^{1}/_{2}$ cup sour cream

salt and pepper

Celery & Bleu Cheese Soup

Melt the butter in a large saucepan over medium–low heat. Add the onion and cook for 3–4 minutes, stirring frequently, until just softened. Add the celery and carrot and continue cooking for 3 minutes. Season lightly with salt and pepper.

Add the stock, thyme, and bay leaf and bring to a boil. Reduce the heat, cover, and simmer gently for about 25 minutes, stirring occasionally, until the vegetables are very tender.

Let the soup cool slightly and remove the thyme and bay leaf. Transfer the soup to a food processor or blender and process until smooth, working in batches, if necessary. (If using a food processor, strain off the cooking liquid and reserve. Purée the soup solids with enough cooking liquid to moisten them, then combine with the remaining liquid.)

Return the puréed soup to the rinsed-out pan and stir in the cream. Simmer over low heat for 5 minutes.

Add the cheese slowly, stirring continuously, until smooth. (Do not allow the soup to boil.) Taste and adjust the seasoning, adding salt, if needed, plenty of pepper, and nutmeg to taste.

Ladle into warmed bowls, garnish with celery leaves, and serve.

SERVES 4

2 tbsp butter

1 onion, finely chopped

4 large celery stalks, finely chopped

1 large carrot, finely chopped

4 cups Chicken Stock (see page 11) or Vegetable Stock (see page 10)

3–4 thyme sprigs

1 bay leaf

$^1/_2$ cup heavy cream

$5^1/_2$ oz/150 g bleu cheese, crumbled

freshly grated nutmeg

salt and pepper

celery leaves, to garnish

White Bean Soup with Olive Tapenade

Pick over the beans, cover generously with cold water, and let soak for 6 hours or overnight. Drain the beans, put in a saucepan, and add cold water to cover by 2 inches/5 cm. Bring to a boil and boil for 10 minutes. Drain and rinse well.

Heat the oil in a large heavy-bottom saucepan over medium heat. Add the onion and leek, cover and cook for 3–4 minutes, stirring occasionally, until just softened. Add the garlic, celery, carrots, and fennel, and continue cooking for 2 minutes.

Add the water, drained beans, and the herbs. When the mixture begins to bubble, reduce the heat to low. Cover and simmer gently, stirring occasionally, for about 1½ hours, until the beans are very tender.

Meanwhile, make the tapenade. Put the garlic, parsley, and drained olives in a food processor or blender with the olive oil. Blend to a purée and scrape into a small serving bowl.

Let the soup cool slightly, then transfer to a food processor or blender and process until smooth, working in batches if necessary. (If using a food processor, strain off the cooking liquid and reserve. Purée the soup solids with enough cooking liquid to moisten them, then combine with the remaining liquid.)

Return the puréed soup to the rinsed-out pan and thin with a little water, if necessary. Season with salt and pepper to taste, and simmer until heated through. Ladle into warmed bowls and serve, stirring a generous teaspoon of the tapenade into each serving.

SERVES 8

12 oz/350 g dried cannellini beans

1 tbsp olive oil

1 large onion, finely chopped

1 large leek (white part only), thinly sliced

3 garlic cloves, finely chopped

2 celery stalks, finely chopped

2 small carrots, finely chopped

1 small fennel bulb, finely chopped

8 cups water

$^1/_4$ tsp dried thyme

$^1/_4$ tsp dried marjoram

salt and pepper

tapenade

1 garlic clove

1 small bunch fresh flat-leaf parsley, stems removed

$8^1/_2$ oz/240 g almond-stuffed green olives, drained

5 tbsp olive oil

Chestnut Soup

Melt the butter in a large saucepan over medium heat. Add the onion and celery and cook for 4–5 minutes, until softened.

Add the chestnuts and sauté for an additional 5 minutes.

Pour in the stock and mix well. Bring to a boil and simmer for 20–25 minutes, until the chestnuts are tender.

Transfer to a food processor or blender and process until smooth. Return to the rinsed-out pan.

Add the cream to the soup, reheat, and season with salt and pepper to taste.

Add the sherry, if using, and serve in warmed bowls, garnished with the parsley.

SERVES 6

2 tbsp butter or 1 tbsp olive oil

1 onion, finely chopped

1 celery stalk, chopped

7 oz/200 g vacuum-packed whole chestnuts

4 cups Chicken Stock (see page 11) or Vegetable Stock (see page 10)

$^1/_2$ cup light cream

2 tbsp sherry (optional)

salt and pepper

chopped fresh parsley, to garnish

Vichyssoise

Trim the leeks and remove most of the green part. Slice the white part of the leeks very finely.

Melt the butter in a saucepan. Add the leeks and onion and cook, stirring occasionally, for about 5 minutes without browning.

Add the potatoes, stock, lemon juice, nutmeg, coriander, and bay leaf to the pan, season with salt and pepper to taste, and bring to a boil. Cover and simmer for about 30 minutes, until all the vegetables are very soft.

Cool the soup a little, remove and discard the bay leaf, and then press through a sieve or process in a food processor or blender until smooth. Pour into a clean saucepan.

Blend the egg yolk into the cream, add a little of the soup to the mixture, and then whisk it all back into the soup and reheat gently, without boiling. Adjust the seasoning to taste. Cool and then chill thoroughly in the refrigerator.

Serve the soup sprinkled with freshly snipped chives.

SERVES 6

3 large leeks

3 tbsp butter or margarine

1 onion, thinly sliced

1 lb/450 g potatoes, chopped

$3^1/_2$ cups Vegetable Stock
  (see page 10)

2 tsp lemon juice

pinch of ground nutmeg

$^1/_4$ tsp ground coriander

1 bay leaf

1 egg yolk

$^2/_3$ cup light cream

salt and white pepper

freshly snipped chives, to garnish

Bloody Mary Soup

Put the tomatoes and stock into a saucepan and cook with the garlic and basil for 3–4 minutes.

Transfer to a food processor or blender and process until smooth. Return to the rinsed-out saucepan.

Season with salt and pepper to taste, Worcestershire sauce, and Tabasco sauce.

Stir in the vodka and serve in small warmed bowls garnished with the parsley. This soup can also be served cold.

SERVES 4

14 oz/400 g canned chopped
  tomatoes
$1^1/_2$ cups Chicken Stock
  (see page 11)
2 garlic cloves, crushed
small handful of basil leaves
Worcestershire sauce
Tabasco sauce, to taste
4 tbsp vodka, to taste
salt and pepper
sprigs of fresh flat-leaf parsley,
  to garnish

Chicken Ravioli in Tarragon Broth

To make the pasta, combine the flour, tarragon, and a pinch of salt in a food processor. Beat together the egg, egg yolk, oil, and 2 tablespoons of the water. With the machine running, pour in the egg mixture and process until it forms a ball, leaving the sides of the bowl virtually clean. If the dough is crumbly, add the remaining water; if the dough is sticky, add 1–2 tablespoons flour and continue kneading in the food processor until a ball forms. Wrap and chill for at least 30 minutes. Reserve the egg white.

To make the filling, put the chicken, lemon rind, and mixed herbs in a food processor and season with salt and pepper. Chop finely by pulsing; do not overprocess. Scrape into a bowl and stir in the cream. Taste and adjust the seasoning, if necessary.

Divide the pasta dough in half. Cover one half and roll the other half on a floured surface as thinly as possible, less than 1/16 inch/ 1.5 mm. Cut out rectangles about 4 x 2 inches/10 x 5 cm. Place rounded teaspoons of filling on one half of the dough pieces. Brush around the edges with egg white and fold in half. Press the edges gently but firmly to seal. Arrange the ravioli in one layer on a baking sheet, dusted generously with flour. Repeat with the remaining dough. Let the ravioli dry in a cool place for about 15 minutes or chill for 1–2 hours.

Bring a large quantity of water to a boil. Drop in half the ravioli and cook for 12–15 minutes, until just tender. Drain on a clean dish towel while cooking the remainder.

Meanwhile, put the stock and tarragon in a large saucepan. Bring to a boil and reduce the heat to bubble very gently. Cover and simmer for about 15 minutes, to infuse. Add the cooked ravioli to the stock and simmer for about 5 minutes until reheated. Ladle into warmed soup bowls to serve.

SERVES 6

8 cups Chicken Stock (see page 11)

2 tbsp finely chopped fresh tarragon leaves

pasta dough

1 cup all-purpose flour, plus extra if needed

2 tbsp fresh tarragon leaves, stems removed

2 eggs, 1 separated

1 tsp extra virgin olive oil

2–3 tbsp water

salt

filling

7 oz/200 g cooked chicken, coarsely chopped

1/2 tsp grated lemon rind

2 tbsp chopped mixed fresh tarragon, chives, and parsley

4 tbsp heavy cream

salt and pepper

Italian Chicken Soup

Place the chicken in a large saucepan and pour in the chicken stock and cream. Bring to a boil, then reduce the heat and simmer for 20 minutes.

Meanwhile, bring a large, heavy-bottom saucepan of lightly salted water to a boil. Add the pasta, return to a boil, and cook for 10–12 minutes, or until just tender but still firm to the bite. Drain the pasta well and keep warm.

Season the soup with salt and pepper to taste. Mix the cornstarch and milk together until a smooth paste forms, then stir it into the soup. Add the corn and pasta and heat through. Ladle the soup into warmed soup bowls and serve.

SERVES 4

1 lb/450 g skinless, boneless chicken breast, cut into thin strips

5 cups Chicken Stock (see page 11)

²/₃ cup heavy cream

4 oz/115 g dried vermicelli

1 tbsp cornstarch

3 tbsp milk

6 oz/175 g canned corn kernels, drained

salt and pepper

Turkey Soup with Rice, Mushrooms & Sage

Melt half the butter in a large saucepan over medium–low heat. Add the onion, celery, and sage and cook for 3–4 minutes, until the onion is softened, stirring frequently. Stir in the flour and continue cooking for 2 minutes.

Slowly add about one quarter of the stock and stir well, scraping the bottom of the pan to mix in the flour. Pour in the remaining stock, stirring to combine completely, and bring just to a boil.

Stir in the rice and season with salt and pepper. Reduce the heat and simmer gently, partially covered, for about 30 minutes until the rice is just tender, stirring occasionally.

Meanwhile, melt the remaining butter in a large skillet over medium heat. Add the mushrooms and season with salt and pepper. Cook for about 8 minutes, until they are golden brown, stirring occasionally at first, then more often after they start to color. Add the mushrooms to the soup.

Add the turkey to the soup and stir in the cream. Continue simmering for about 10 minutes, until heated through. Taste and adjust the seasoning, if necessary. Ladle into warmed bowls, garnish with sage, and serve with Parmesan cheese.

SERVES 4–5

3 tbsp butter

1 onion, finely chopped

1 celery stalk, finely chopped

25 large fresh sage leaves, finely chopped

4 tbsp all-purpose flour

5 cups turkey stock or Chicken Stock (see page 11)

$^2/_3$ cup brown rice

9 oz/250 g mushrooms, sliced

7 oz/200 g cooked turkey

$^3/_4$ cup heavy cream

salt and pepper

sprigs of fresh sage, to garnish

freshly grated Parmesan cheese, to serve

Lemon Turkey Soup with Mushrooms

Put the turkey in a large saucepan and add the stock. Bring just to a boil and skim off any foam that rises to the surface.

Add the onion, carrots, garlic, lemon rind, and bay leaf. Season with salt and pepper. Reduce the heat and simmer, partially covered, for about 45 minutes, stirring occasionally, until the turkey is cooked.

Remove the turkey and carrots with a slotted spoon and reserve, covered. Strain the stock into a clean saucepan. Discard the onion, garlic, lemon rind, and bay leaf.

Melt the butter in a skillet over medium–high heat. Add the mushrooms, season with salt and pepper, and cook gently until lightly golden. Reserve with the turkey and carrots.

Mix together the cornstarch and cream. Bring the cooking liquid just to a boil and whisk in the cream mixture. Boil very gently for 2–3 minutes until it thickens, whisking almost continuously.

Add the reserved meat and vegetables to the soup and simmer over low heat for about 5 minutes until heated through. Taste and adjust the seasoning, adding nutmeg and a squeeze of lemon juice, if using. Stir in the parsley, then ladle into warmed bowls and serve.

SERVES 4–5

12 oz/350 g boneless turkey, cut into $1/2$-inch/1-cm pieces

4 cups chicken stock

1 onion, quartered

2 carrots, thinly sliced

2 garlic cloves, halved

1 pared strip lemon rind

1 bay leaf

1 tbsp butter

12 oz/350 g small button mushrooms, quartered

4 tbsp cornstarch

$1/2$ cup heavy cream

freshly grated nutmeg

fresh lemon juice, to taste (optional)

1–2 tbsp chopped fresh parsley

salt and pepper

Tuscan Veal Broth

Put the peas, veal, stock, and water into a large saucepan and bring to a boil over low heat. Using a slotted spoon, skim off any foam that rises to the surface.

When all of the foam has been removed, add the pearl barley and a pinch of salt to the mixture. Simmer gently over low heat for 25 minutes.

Add the carrot, turnip, leek, onion, tomatoes, and basil to the pan, and season with salt and pepper to taste. Simmer for about 2 hours, skimming the surface from time to time to remove any foam. Remove the pan from the heat and set aside for 2 hours.

Set the pan over medium heat and bring to a boil. Add the vermicelli and cook for 8–10 minutes. Season with salt and pepper to taste; remove and discard the basil. Ladle into warmed bowls and serve immediately.

SERVES 4

$^1/_3$ cup dried peas, soaked for 2 hours and drained

2 lb/900 g boned neck of veal, diced

5 cups Beef Stock (see page 11)

$2^1/_2$ cups water

$^1/_3$ cup pearl barley, washed

1 large carrot, diced

1 small turnip (about 6 oz/175 g), diced

1 large leek, thinly sliced

1 red onion, finely chopped

$3^1/_2$ oz/100 g chopped tomatoes

1 fresh basil sprig

3 oz/85 g dried vermicelli

salt and pepper

Asian Pork Meatballs & Greens in Broth

To make the pork meatballs, put the pork, spinach, scallions, and garlic in a bowl. Add the 5-spice powder and soy sauce and mix until combined.

Shape the pork mixture into 24 meatballs. Place them in one layer in a steamer that will fit over the top of a saucepan.

Bring the stock just to a boil in a saucepan that will accommodate the steamer. Regulate the heat so that the liquid bubbles gently. Add the mushrooms to the stock and place the steamer, covered, on top of the pan. Steam for 10 minutes. Remove the steamer and set aside on a plate.

Add the bok choy and scallions to the pan and cook gently in the stock for 3–4 minutes, or until the leaves are wilted. Taste the soup and adjust the seasoning, if necessary.

Divide the pork meatballs evenly among 6 warmed bowls and ladle the soup over them. Serve immediately.

SERVES 6

8 cups Chicken Stock (see page 11)
3 oz/85 g shiitake mushrooms, thinly sliced
6 oz/175 g bok choy or other Asian greens, sliced into thin ribbons
6 scallions, finely sliced
salt and pepper

pork meatballs

8 oz/225 g fresh lean ground pork
1 oz/25 g fresh spinach leaves, finely chopped
2 scallions, finely chopped
1 garlic clove, very finely chopped
pinch of Chinese 5-spice powder
1 tsp soy sauce

Consommé

Put the stock and ground beef in a saucepan and set aside for 1 hour. Add the tomatoes, carrots, onion, celery, turnip (if using), bouquet garni, 2 of the egg whites, the crushed shells of 2 of the eggs, and plenty of seasoning. Bring almost to boiling point, whisking hard all the time with a flat whisk.

Cover and simmer for 1 hour, taking care not to allow the layer of froth on top of the soup to break.

Pour the soup through a colander lined with two layers of cheesecloth, keeping the froth back until the end, then pour the ingredients through the cloth again into a clean saucepan. The resulting liquid should be clear.

If the soup is not quite clear, return it to the pan with another egg white and the crushed shells of 2 more eggs. Repeat the whisking process as before and then boil for 10 minutes; strain again.

Add the sherry, if using, to the soup and reheat gently. Place the garnish in warmed soup bowls and carefully pour in the soup. Serve immediately.

SERVES 4–6

5 cups Rich Beef Stock
(see page 176)

1 cup fresh extra-lean ground beef

2 tomatoes, peeled, seeded, and
chopped

2 large carrots, chopped

1 large onion, chopped

2 celery stalks, chopped

1 turnip, chopped (optional)

1 bouquet garni

2–3 egg whites

shells of 2–4 eggs, crushed

1–2 tbsp sherry (optional)

salt and pepper

julienne strips of raw carrot, turnip,
celery, or celery root, to garnish

Tomato Broth with Angel Hair Pasta

Put the tomatoes, garlic cloves, onion, saffron, sugar, bouquet garni, and lemon rind into a large, heavy-bottom saucepan. Pour in the stock and bring to a boil, then reduce the heat, cover, and simmer, stirring occasionally, for 25–30 minutes, until the tomatoes have disintegrated.

Remove the pan from the heat and let cool slightly. Remove and discard the garlic cloves, bouquet garni, and lemon rind. Ladle the tomato mixture into a food processor or blender and process to a purée.

Return the purée to the rinsed-out pan and season with salt and pepper to taste. Stir in the olive oil and bring to a boil. Add the pasta, bring back to a boil, and cook for 2–4 minutes, until tender but still firm to the bite.

Taste and adjust the seasoning, if necessary. Ladle the broth and pasta into warmed soup bowls and serve immediately.

SERVES 4

1 lb 2 oz/500 g ripe tomatoes, peeled and halved

8 garlic cloves, peeled but left whole

1 onion, chopped

$^1/_2$ tsp saffron threads, lightly crushed

1 tsp sugar

1 bouquet garni

2-inch/5-cm strip thinly pared lemon rind

$2^1/_2$ cups Vegetable Stock (see page 10) or Chicken Stock (see page 11)

2 tbsp extra virgin olive oil

10 oz/280 g dried angel hair pasta

salt and pepper

Cold Cucumber & Smoked Salmon Soup

Heat the oil in a large saucepan over medium heat. Add the onion and cook for about 3 minutes, until it begins to soften.

Add the cucumber, potato, celery, and stock. Bring to a boil, reduce the heat, cover, and cook gently for about 20 minutes, until the vegetables are tender.

Let the soup cool slightly, then transfer to a food processor or blender, working in batches if necessary. Purée the soup until smooth. (If using a food processor, strain off the cooking liquid and reserve it. Purée the soup solids with enough cooking liquid to moisten them, then combine with the remaining liquid.)

Transfer the puréed soup to a large container. Cover and refrigerate until cold.

Stir the cream, salmon, and chives into the soup. If time permits, chill for at least 1 hour to allow the flavors to blend. Taste and adjust the seasoning, adding salt, if needed, and pepper. Ladle into chilled bowls and serve.

SERVES 4

2 tsp olive oil

1 large onion, finely chopped

1 large cucumber, peeled, seeded, and sliced

1 small potato, diced

1 celery stalk, finely chopped

4 cups Chicken Stock (see page 11) or Vegetable Stock (see page 10)

$1^2/_3$ cups heavy cream

$5^1/_2$ oz/150 g smoked salmon, finely diced

2 tbsp snipped fresh chives

salt and pepper

Bouillabaisse

Heat the oil in a large saucepan over medium heat. Add the garlic and onions and cook, stirring, for 3 minutes. Stir in the tomatoes, stock, wine, bay leaf, saffron, and herbs. Bring to a boil, reduce the heat, cover, and simmer for 30 minutes.

Meanwhile, soak the mussels in lightly salted water for 10 minutes. Scrub the shells under cold running water and pull off any beards. Discard any mussels with broken shells or any that refuse to close when tapped. Put the rest into a large saucepan with a little water, bring to a boil, and cook over high heat for 4 minutes. Remove from the heat and discard any that remain closed.

When the tomato mixture is cooked, rinse the fish, pat dry, and cut into chunks. Add to the pan and simmer for 5 minutes. Add the mussels, shrimp, and scallops, and season with salt and pepper to taste. Cook for 3 minutes, until the fish is cooked through. Remove from the heat, discard the bay leaf, and ladle into warmed bowls.

SERVES 4

scant $^1/_2$ cup olive oil

3 garlic cloves, chopped

2 onions, chopped

2 tomatoes, seeded and chopped

$2^3/_4$ cups Fish Stock (see page 10)

$1^3/_4$ cups white wine

1 bay leaf

pinch of saffron threads

2 tbsp chopped fresh basil

2 tbsp chopped fresh parsley

7 oz/200 g live mussels

9 oz/250 g red snapper fillets or monkfish fillets

9 oz/250 g cod fillets, skinned

7 oz/200 g shrimp, peeled and deveined

$3^1/_2$ oz/100 g scallops

salt and pepper

Seared Scallops in Garlic Broth

Combine the garlic cloves, celery, carrot, onion, peppercorns, parsley stems, and water in a saucepan with a good pinch of salt. Bring to a boil, reduce the heat, and simmer, partially covered, for 30–45 minutes.

Strain the stock into a clean saucepan. Taste and adjust the seasoning, and keep hot.

If using sea scallops, slice in half to form 2 thinner rounds from each. (If the scallops are very large, slice them into 3 rounds.) Sprinkle with salt and pepper.

Heat the oil in a skillet over medium–high heat and cook the scallops on one side for 1–2 minutes, until lightly browned and the flesh becomes opaque.

Divide the scallops among 4 warmed shallow bowls, arranging them browned-side up. Ladle the soup over the scallops, then float a few cilantro leaves on top. Serve immediately.

SERVES 4

1 large garlic bulb (about $3^1/2$ oz/ 100 g), separated into unpeeled cloves

1 celery stalk, chopped

1 carrot, chopped

1 onion, chopped

10 peppercorns

5–6 parsley stems

5 cups water

8 oz/225 g large sea scallops

1 tbsp oil

salt and pepper

fresh cilantro leaves, to garnish

Saffron Mussel Soup

Discard any mussels with broken shells or any that refuse to close when tapped. Rinse, pull off any beards, and if there are barnacles, scrape them off with a knife under cold running water.

Put the mussels in a large, heavy-bottom saucepan over high heat with the wine and a little pepper. Cover tightly and cook for 4–5 minutes, or until the mussels open, shaking the pan occasionally. Discard any that remain closed.

When they are cool enough to handle, remove the mussels from the shells, adding any additional juices to the cooking liquid. Strain the cooking liquid through a cheesecloth-lined sieve. Top up the cooking liquid with water to make 4 cups.

Melt the butter in a heavy-bottom saucepan. Add the shallots and leek, cover, and cook until they begin to soften, stirring occasionally.

Stir in the mussel cooking liquid and the saffron. Bring to a boil, reduce the heat, and simmer for 15–20 minutes, until the vegetables are very tender.

Add the cream, stir, and bring just to a boil. Stir the dissolved cornstarch into the soup and boil gently for 2–3 minutes, until slightly thickened, stirring frequently. Add the mussels and cook for 1–2 minutes to reheat them. Taste and adjust the seasoning, if necessary. Stir in the parsley, ladle into warmed bowls, and serve.

SERVES 4–6

4 lb 8 oz/2 kg live mussels

$^2/_3$ cup dry white wine

1 tbsp butter

2 large shallots, finely chopped

1 leek, halved lengthwise and thinly sliced

pinch of saffron threads

$1^1/_4$ cups heavy cream

1 tbsp cornstarch, dissolved in 2 tbsp water

2 tbsp chopped fresh parsley

salt and pepper

Squid, Chorizo & Tomato Soup

Cut off the squid tentacles and cut into bite-size pieces. Slice the bodies into rings.

Place a large saucepan over medium–low heat and add the chorizo. Cook for 5–10 minutes, stirring frequently, until it renders most of its fat. Remove with a slotted spoon and drain on paper towels.

Pour off all the fat from the pan and add the onion, celery, carrot, and garlic. Cover and cook for 3–4 minutes, until the onion is slightly softened.

Stir in the tomatoes, stock, cumin, saffron, bay leaf, and chorizo.

Add the squid to the soup. Bring almost to a boil, reduce the heat, cover, and cook gently, stirring occasionally, for 40–45 minutes, or until the squid and carrot are tender.

Taste the soup and stir in a little chili paste for a spicier flavor, if using. Season with salt and pepper. Ladle into warmed bowls, sprinkle with parsley, and serve.

SERVES 6

1 lb/450 g cleaned squid

$5^1/_2$ oz/150 g lean chorizo sausage, peeled and very finely diced

1 onion, finely chopped

1 celery stalk, thinly sliced

1 carrot, thinly sliced

2 garlic cloves, finely chopped or crushed

14 oz/400 g canned chopped tomatoes

5 cups Fish Stock (see page 10)

$^1/_2$ tsp ground cumin

pinch of saffron

1 bay leaf

chili paste (optional)

salt and pepper

fresh chopped parsley, to garnish

Crab & Vegetable Soup

Heat the oil in a large saucepan over medium heat. Add the garlic and scallions and cook, stirring, for about 3 minutes, until slightly softened. Add the bell peppers and ginger and cook for another 4 minutes, stirring. Pour in the stock and season with salt and pepper. Bring to a boil, then reduce the heat. Pour in the coconut milk, rice wine, and lime juice and stir in the grated lime zest and kaffir lime leaves. Simmer for 15 minutes.

Add the crabmeat and crab claws to the soup with the corn and cilantro. Cook the soup for 15 minutes, until the fish is tender and cooked right through.

Remove from the heat and ladle into warmed bowls. Garnish with fresh cilantro and serve.

SERVES 4

2 tbsp chili oil

1 garlic clove, chopped

4 scallions, trimmed and sliced

2 red bell peppers, seeded and chopped

1 tbsp grated fresh ginger

4 cups Fish Stock (see page 10)

scant $^{1}/_{2}$ cup coconut milk

scant $^{1}/_{2}$ cup rice wine or sherry

2 tbsp lime juice

1 tbsp grated lime zest

6 kaffir lime leaves, finely shredded

$10^{1}/_{2}$ oz/300 g freshly cooked crabmeat

7 oz/200 g freshly cooked crab claws

$5^{1}/_{2}$ oz/150 g canned corn kernels, drained

1 tbsp chopped cilantro, plus a few sprigs to garnish

salt and pepper

Mussel & Pasta Soup

Discard any mussels with broken shells or any that refuse to close when tapped. Bring a large, heavy-bottom saucepan of water to a boil. Add the mussels and oil and season with pepper to taste. Cover tightly and cook over high heat for 5 minutes, or until the mussels have opened. Remove the mussels with a slotted spoon, discarding any that remain closed. Strain the cooking liquid and set aside 5 cups.

Melt the butter in a clean saucepan. Add the bacon, onion, and garlic, and cook over low heat, stirring occasionally, for 5 minutes. Stir in the flour and cook, stirring, for 1 minute. Gradually stir in all but 2 tablespoons of the reserved cooking liquid and bring to a boil, stirring continuously. Add the potato slices and simmer for 5 minutes. Add the pasta and simmer for an additional 10 minutes.

Stir in the cream and lemon juice and season with salt and pepper to taste. Add the mussels. Mix the egg yolks and the remaining mussel cooking liquid together, then stir the mixture into the soup and cook for 4 minutes, until thickened.
Ladle the soup into warmed soup bowls, garnish with chopped parsley, and serve immediately.

SERVES 4

1 lb 10 oz/750 g mussels, scrubbed
  and debearded

2 tbsp olive oil

$^1/_2$ cup butter

2 oz/55 g rindless lean bacon,
  chopped

1 onion, chopped

2 garlic cloves, finely chopped

$^3/_8$ cup all-purpose flour

3 potatoes, thinly sliced

4 oz/115 g dried farfalle
  (pasta bows)

1$^1/_4$ cups heavy cream

1 tbsp lemon juice

2 egg yolks

salt and pepper

2 tbsp finely chopped fresh parsley,
  to garnish

Lobster Bisque

Pull off the lobster tail. With the legs up, cut the body in half lengthwise. Scoop out the tomalley (the soft pale greenish-gray part) and, if it is a female, the roe (the solid red-orange part). Reserve these together, covered and refrigerated. Remove the meat and cut into bite-size pieces; cover and refrigerate. Chop the shell into large pieces.

Melt half the butter in a large saucepan over medium heat and add the lobster shell pieces. Cook until brown bits begin to stick on the bottom of the pan. Add the carrot, celery, leek, onion, and shallots. Cook, stirring, for 1½–2 minutes (do not let it burn). Add the brandy and wine and bubble for 1 minute. Pour over the water, add the tomato paste and a large pinch of salt, and bring to a boil. Reduce the heat, simmer for 30 minutes, and strain the stock, discarding the solids.

Melt the remaining butter in a small saucepan and add the tomalley and roe, if any. Add the cream, whisk to mix well, remove from the heat, and set aside.

Put the flour in a small mixing bowl and very slowly whisk in the cold water. Stir in a little of the hot stock mixture to make a smooth liquid.

Bring the remaining lobster stock to a boil and whisk in the flour mixture. Boil gently for 4–5 minutes until the soup thickens, stirring frequently. Press the tomalley, roe, and cream mixture through a sieve into the soup. Reduce the heat and add the reserved lobster meat. Simmer gently until heated through.

Taste the soup and adjust the seasoning, adding more cream if desired. Ladle into warmed bowls, sprinkle with chives, and serve.

SERVES 4

1 lb/450 g cooked lobster

3 tbsp butter

1 small carrot, grated

1 celery stalk, finely chopped

1 leek, finely chopped

1 small onion, finely chopped

2 shallots, finely chopped

3 tbsp brandy or cognac

¼ cup dry white wine

5 cups water

1 tbsp tomato paste

½ cup heavy cream, or to taste

6 tbsp all-purpose flour

2–3 tbsp water

salt and pepper

snipped fresh chives, to garnish

Shrimp & Vegetable Bisque

Melt the butter in a large saucepan over medium heat. Add the garlic and onion and cook, stirring, for 3 minutes, until slightly softened. Add the carrot and celery and cook for another 3 minutes, stirring. Pour in the stock and red wine, then add the tomato paste and bay leaf. Season with salt and pepper. Bring to a boil, then reduce the heat and simmer for 20 minutes. Remove from the heat and let cool for 10 minutes, then remove and discard the bay leaf.

Transfer half of the soup to a food processor and blend until smooth (you may need to do this in batches). Return to the pan with the rest of the soup. Add the shrimp and cook the soup over low heat for 5–6 minutes.

Stir in the cream and cook for another 2 minutes, then remove from the heat and ladle into warmed bowls. Garnish with swirls of light cream and whole cooked shrimp, and serve at once.

SERVES 4

3 tbsp butter

1 garlic clove, chopped

1 onion, sliced

1 carrot, peeled and chopped

1 celery stalk, trimmed and sliced

5 cups Fish Stock (see page 10)

4 tbsp red wine

1 tbsp tomato paste

1 bay leaf

1 lb 5 oz/600 g shrimp, peeled and
   deveined

scant $^1/_2$ cup heavy cream

salt and pepper

swirls of single cream and whole
   cooked shrimp, to garnish

Creamy Oyster Soup

To open the oysters, hold flat-side up, over a sieve set over a bowl to catch the juices, and push an oyster knife into the hinge. Work it around until you can pry off the top shell. When all the oysters have been opened, strain the liquid through a sieve lined with damp cheesecloth. Remove any bits of shell stuck to the oysters and reserve them in their liquid.

Melt half the butter in a saucepan over low heat. Add the shallots and cook gently for about 5 minutes, until just softened, stirring frequently; do not allow them to brown.

Add the wine, bring to a boil, and boil for 1 minute. Stir in the fish stock, bring back to a boil, and boil for 3–4 minutes. Reduce the heat to a gentle simmer.

Add the oysters and their liquid and poach for about 1 minute, until they become more firm but are still tender. Remove the oysters with a slotted spoon and reserve, covered. Strain the stock.

Bring the strained stock to a boil in a clean saucepan. Add the cream and bring back to a boil.

Stir the dissolved cornstarch into the soup and boil gently for 2–3 minutes, stirring frequently, until slightly thickened. Add the oysters and cook for 1–2 minutes to reheat them. Taste and adjust the seasoning, if necessary, and ladle the soup into warmed bowls. Top each serving with a teaspoon of caviar or roe, if using.

SERVES 4

12 oysters

2 tbsp butter

2 shallots, finely chopped

5 tbsp white wine

$1^{1}/_{4}$ cups Fish Stock (see page 10)

$^{3}/_{4}$ cup heavy cream

2 tbsp cornstarch, dissolved in
    2 tbsp cold water

salt and pepper

caviar or lumpfish roe, to garnish
    (optional)

6

Accompaniments

Freshly baked bread is the perfect partner for homemade soup—it is ideal for dunking and for mopping up the last delicious drops. Any leftover bread can be used to make croutons, adding taste and crunch. Croutons can be made in a variety of flavors, such as garlic, chile, or herb, to provide a perfect complement to the soup they are accompanying.

Croutons

Cut the bread into $1/2$-inch/1-cm cubes.

Heat the oil in a skillet, add the garlic, if using, and cook for 1 minute. Add the bread cubes in a single layer, tossing occasionally, until they are golden brown and crisp.

Remove the skillet from the heat and spoon the croutons onto paper towels to drain.

While the croutons are still hot, toss them in the fresh herbs, paprika, or Parmesan cheese, if using. Season with salt and pepper to taste.

The croutons are best used on the day of making.

SERVES 4–6

2 slices day-old white, whole wheat, or whole grain bread, crusts removed

4 tbsp vegetable or olive oil

1 garlic clove, finely chopped (optional)

finely chopped fresh herbs, such as parsley and thyme (optional)

$1/2$ teaspoon paprika or chili powder (optional)

1 tbsp freshly grated Parmesan cheese (optional)

salt and pepper

White Bread

Mix the flour, salt, and yeast together in a mixing bowl. Add the oil and water and stir well to form a soft dough.

Turn out the dough onto a lightly floured board and knead well by hand for 5–7 minutes. Alternatively, use a freestanding electric mixer for this and knead the dough with the dough hook for 4–5 minutes. The dough should have a smooth appearance and feel elastic.

Return the dough to the bowl, cover with plastic wrap, and let rise in a warm place for 1 hour. When it has doubled in size, turn it out onto a floured board and knead again for 30 seconds; this is known as "punching down." Knead it until smooth.

Shape the dough into a rectangle the length of a 2-lb/900-g loaf pan and three times the width. Grease the pan well, fold the dough into three lengthwise, and put it in the pan with the seam underneath for a well-shaped loaf. Cover and let rise in a warm place for 30 minutes, until it has risen well above the pan. Meanwhile, preheat the oven to 425°F/220°C.

Bake in the center of the preheated oven for 25–30 minutes, until firm and golden brown. Test that the loaf is cooked by tapping it on the bottom—it should sound hollow. Cool on a wire rack for 30 minutes.

MAKES 1 LARGE LOAF

4 cups white bread flour, plus extra for dusting

1 tsp salt

$1/4$ oz/7 g active dry yeast

1 tbsp vegetable oil or melted butter, plus extra for greasing

$1^{1}/_{4}$ cups lukewarm water

Irish Soda Bread

Preheat the oven to 450°F/230°C, then dust a cookie sheet with flour. Sift the flours, baking soda, and salt into a bowl and stir in the sugar. Make a well in the center and pour in enough of the buttermilk to make a dough that is soft but not too wet and sticky. Add a little more buttermilk, if necessary.

Turn out the dough onto a floured counter and knead very briefly into a large circle, 2 inches/5 cm thick. Dust lightly with flour and, using a sharp knife, mark the top of the loaf with a deep cross.

Place the loaf on the cookie sheet and bake in the preheated oven for 15 minutes. Reduce the oven temperature to 400°F/200°C and bake for an additional 20–25 minutes, or until the loaf sounds hollow when tapped on the bottom. Transfer to a wire rack to cool, and eat while still warm.

MAKES 1 LOAF

2 cups white all-purpose flour, plus extra for dusting

2 cups whole wheat flour

$1^1/_2$ tsp baking soda

1 tsp salt

1 tsp brown sugar

$1^3/_4$ cups buttermilk

Chile Cheese Cornbread

Preheat the oven to 400°F/200°C. Grease a heavy-bottom 9-inch/ 23-cm cake pan or ovenproof skillet and line the bottom with waxed paper. Sift the flour, baking powder, and salt into a bowl, then stir in the cornmeal and a cup of the grated cheese.

Pour the melted butter into a bowl and stir in the eggs and milk. Pour onto the dry ingredients, add the chile, then mix quickly until just combined. Do not overmix.

Spoon the mixture into the prepared pan, scatter the remaining cheese on top, and bake in the preheated oven for 20 minutes, or until risen and golden. Let cool in the pan for 2 minutes, then turn out onto a wire rack to cool completely.

MAKES 1 LOAF

$^3/_4$ cup self-rising flour

1 tbsp baking powder

1 tsp salt

$1^1/_2$ cups fine cornmeal

$1^1/_2$ cups grated sharp cheddar cheese

4 tbsp butter, melted, plus extra for greasing

2 eggs, beaten

$1^1/_4$ cups milk

1 fresh red chile, seeded and finely chopped

Herb Focaccia

Combine the flour, yeast, salt, and sugar in a bowl and make a well in the center. Gradually stir in most of the water and 2 tablespoons of the oil to make a dough. Gradually add the remaining water, if necessary, drawing in all the flour.

Turn out onto a lightly floured counter and knead. Transfer to a bowl and lightly knead in the herbs for 10 minutes, until soft but not sticky. Wash the bowl and lightly coat with oil.

Shape the dough into a ball, put it in the bowl, and turn the dough over so it is coated with oil. Cover tightly with a dish towel or lightly greased plastic wrap and let rise in a warm place until the dough has doubled in volume. Meanwhile, sprinkle cornmeal over a cookie sheet.

Turn out the dough onto a lightly floured counter and knead lightly. Cover with the upturned bowl and let stand for 10 minutes. Meanwhile, preheat the oven to 450°F/230°C.

Roll out and pat the dough into a 10-inch/25-cm circle, about ½ inch/1 cm thick, and carefully transfer it to the prepared cookie sheet. Cover with a dish towel and let rise again for 15 minutes.

Using a lightly oiled finger, poke indentations all over the surface of the loaf. Drizzle over the remaining oil and sprinkle lightly with sea salt. Bake in the preheated oven for 15 minutes, or until golden brown and the loaf sounds hollow when tapped on the bottom. Transfer to a wire rack to cool completely.

MAKES 1 LOAF

3½ cups white bread flour, plus extra for dusting

¼ oz/7 g active dry yeast

1½ tsp salt

½ tsp sugar

1¼ cups lukewarm water

3 tbsp extra virgin olive oil, plus extra for greasing

4 tbsp finely chopped fresh mixed herbs

cornmeal, for sprinkling

sea salt, for sprinkling

Olive Rolls

Pit the olives with an olive or cherry pitter and finely chop. Pat off the excess brine or oil with paper towels. Set aside.

Combine the flour, salt, and yeast in a bowl and make a well in the center. Gradually stir in most of the water and the oil to make a dough. Gradually add the remaining water, if necessary, drawing in all the flour.

Lightly knead in the chopped olives and herbs. Turn out the dough onto a lightly floured counter and knead for 10 minutes, until smooth and elastic. Wash the bowl and lightly coat with oil.

Shape the dough into a ball, put it in the bowl, and turn over so it is coated with oil. Cover tightly with a dish towel or lightly oiled plastic wrap and leave to rise until it has doubled in volume. Meanwhile, preheat the oven to 425°F/220°C and dust a cookie sheet with flour.

Turn out the dough onto a lightly floured counter and knead lightly. Roll the dough into 8-inch/20-cm sausages.

Cut the dough into 16 even-size pieces. Shape each piece into a ball and place on the prepared cookie sheet. Cover and let rise for 15 minutes.

Lightly brush the top of each roll with olive oil. Bake in the preheated oven for about 25–30 minutes, or until the rolls are golden brown. Transfer to a wire rack and set aside to cool completely.

MAKES 16 ROLLS

1 cup olives in brine or oil, drained

$6^1/_2$ cups white bread flour, plus extra for dusting

$1^1/_2$ tsp salt

$^1/_4$ oz/7 g active dry yeast

2 cups lukewarm water

2 tbsp extra virgin olive oil, plus extra for brushing

4 tbsp finely chopped fresh oregano, parsley, or thyme leaves, or 1 tbsp dried mixed herbs

French Baguettes

Sift the flour and salt together into a bowl and stir in the yeast. Make a well in the center and pour in the lukewarm water. Stir well with a wooden spoon until the dough begins to come together, then knead with your hands until it leaves the side of the bowl. Turn out onto a lightly floured counter and knead well for about 10 minutes, until smooth and elastic.

Brush a bowl with oil. Shape the dough into a ball, put it into the bowl, and put the bowl into a plastic bag or cover with a damp dish towel. Let rise in a warm place for 1 hour, until the dough has doubled in volume.

Turn out the dough onto a lightly floured counter, punch down with your fist, and knead for 1–2 minutes. Cut the dough in half and shape each piece into a ball. Roll out each ball to a rectangle measuring 3 x 8 inches/7.5 x 20 cm. From one long side of a dough rectangle, fold one third of the dough down, then fold over the remaining third of the dough. Press gently. Fold the second dough rectangle in the same way. Put both loaves in plastic bags and let rest for 10 minutes. Repeat the rolling and folding twice more, letting the dough rest for 10 minutes each time.

Lightly flour and pleat 2 dish towels. Gently roll and stretch each piece of dough until it is 12 inches/30 cm long and an even thickness. Support each loaf on the pleated dish towels, cover with damp dish towels, and let rise for 30–40 minutes.

Preheat the oven to 450°F/230°C. Brush 1 or 2 cookie sheets with oil. Carefully roll the loaves onto the cookie sheets and slash the tops several times with a sharp knife. Spray the oven with water and bake the loaves for 15–20 minutes, until golden brown. Transfer to a wire rack to cool.

MAKES 2 LOAVES

4 cups white bread flour, plus extra for dusting

1¹/₂ tsp salt

1¹/₂ tsp active dry yeast

1¹/₃ cups lukewarm water

vegetable oil, for brushing

Ciabatta

First, make the biga. Sift the flour into a bowl, stir in the yeast, and make a well in the center. Pour in the lukewarm water and stir until the dough comes together. Turn out onto a lightly floured counter and knead for 5 minutes, until smooth and elastic. Shape the dough into a ball, put it into a bowl, and put the bowl into a plastic bag or cover with a damp dish towel. Let rise in a warm place for 12 hours, until just beginning to collapse.

Gradually mix the water and milk into the biga, beating with a wooden spoon. Gradually mix in the flour and yeast with your hand, adding them a little at a time. Finally, mix in the salt and oil with your hand. The dough will be very wet; do not add extra flour. Put the bowl into a plastic bag or cover with a damp dish towel and let the dough rise in a warm place for 2 hours, until doubled in volume.

Dust 3 cookie sheets with flour. Using a spatula, divide the dough among the prepared cookie sheets without knocking out the air. With lightly floured hands, gently pull and shape each piece of dough into a rectangular loaf, then flatten slightly. Dust the tops of the loaves with flour and let rise in a warm place for 30 minutes.

Meanwhile, preheat the oven to 425°F/220°C. Bake the loaves for 25–30 minutes, until the crust is lightly golden and the loaves sound hollow when tapped on the bottom with your knuckles. Transfer to wire racks to cool.

MAKES 3 LOAVES

$1^3/_4$ cups lukewarm water

4 tbsp lukewarm lowfat milk

$4^1/_2$ cups white bread flour

1 envelope active dry yeast

2 tsp salt

3 tbsp olive oil

biga

3 cups white bread flour, plus extra for dusting

$1^1/_4$ tsp active dry yeast

scant 1 cup lukewarm water